Does Private Sector Participation Improve Performance in Electricity and Water Distribution?

TRENDS AND POLICY OPTIONS ▣ No. 6

HELPING TO ELIMINATE POVERTY THROUGH PRIVATE INVOLVEMENT IN INFRASTRUCTURE

Does Private Sector Participation Improve Performance in Electricity and Water Distribution?

Katharina Gassner
Alexander Popov
Nataliya Pushak

THE WORLD BANK

PPIAF
PUBLIC-PRIVATE INFRASTRUCTURE ADVISORY FACILITY

1818 H Street NW
Washington DC 20433
Telephone: 202-473-1000
Internet: www.worldbank.org
E-mail: feedback@worldbank.org

1 2 3 4 12 11 10 09

ISBN 978-0-8213-7715-4
eISBN: 978-0-8213-7717-8
DOI: 10.1596/978-0-8213-7715-4

Library of Congress Cataloging-in-Publication Data

Gassner, Katharina.

Does private sector participation improve performance in electricity and water distribution? / Katharina Gassner, Alexander Popov, and Nataliya Pushak.

p. cm. -- (Trends and policy options ; no. 6)

Includes bibliographical references and index.

ISBN 978-0-8213-7715-4 -- ISBN 978-0-8213-7717-8 (electronic)

1. Public utilities--Management--Evaluation. 2. Electric utilities--Management. 3. Water utilities--Management. 4. Public-private sector cooperation. I. Popov, Alexander A. II. Pushak, Nataliya. III. World Bank. IV. Title.

HD2763.G36 2008

333.793'2--dc22

2008037293

Cover: Naylor Design, Inc.

CONTENTS

FIGURES

TABLES

FOREWORD

The debate surrounding the operation of utility networks by private companies has a long history. Numerous studies have examined the arguments put forward, often passionately, by proponents of public management and private participation alike, but clear answers have proved elusive for several reasons. Utility services are by their very nature different from other goods and services delivered in competitive markets: they display natural monopoly characteristics and figure prominently in the political and social discourse of governments. The question of whether privately or publicly run utilities perform better is especially difficult to answer in developing countries, where weak legal and institutional environments must be taken into account and data are scarce.

Understanding the tradeoffs between public and private management is critical for policy makers and their advisors. The private sector has long been advocated as a solution to the service delivery gap faced by developing countries, but the wide range of results observed case by case has led to strong feelings both for and against private involvement in utility services.

This study addresses the question with a rigorous econometric approach and distills global results from a multitude of evidence. The data set compiled is unique in its coverage, size, and composition, making it possible to address for the first time methodological problems that have plagued empirical research and hampered conclusive results. The findings provide some answers, but also indicate where the challenges lie going forward. Privately run water and electricity utilities outperform comparable state-owned companies in terms of labor productivity and operational efficiency, but staff reductions also occur. Policy makers need to be aware of and acknowledge both the benefits and the costs of reform. Clear communication between stakeholders plays an important role in the acceptance and success of private participation, and a strategy for mitigating labor issues should be an integral part of reform efforts.

The study also makes it clear that the investment problem is not solved by private participation alone, and it raises questions about the scope for increasing residential tariffs in low-income countries and thus the long-term sustainability of improvements in service delivery, be it by public or private operators.

We hope the work will provide useful insights for policy makers, investors, official agencies, and other stakeholders and will inspire future research into the different ways to increase access to and improve the delivery of water and electricity services in developing countries.

Laszlo Lovei
Director
Finance, Economics and Urban Department
World Bank

Jyoti Shukla
Program Manager
Public-Private Infrastructure Advisory Facility
World Bank

ACKNOWLEDGMENTS

Generous funding from the Public-Private Infrastructure Advisory Facility (PPIAF) has made this research possible and is gratefully acknowledged.

The authors thank Jose Aceves, Carolina Czastkiewicz, and Julio A. Gonzalez for outstanding research assistance. Yanliang Miao, Princeton University, provided valuable input on East Asia, particularly China. Doug Andrew played an important role in the design and implementation of the research. The original idea for the study was based on work by J. Luis Guasch, Vivien Foster, and Luis Andrés for the World Bank's Latin America and the Caribbean Region. Their input in the form of knowledge transfer, data for this region, and final review comments is gratefully acknowledged. Additional review comments were received from Daniel Benitez, Antonio Estache, Eric Groom, Clive Harris, Atsushi Iimi, Tim Irwin, Ada Karina Izaguirre, Mark Schaffer, and especially Clemencia Torres de Mästle and John Nellis. All remaining errors are the authors'.

Many individuals inside and outside the World Bank helped to compile the data on which this report is based, generously offering their knowledge and their contacts. Without their help, this study could not have been undertaken.

Collaboration with the team at the International Benchmarking Network for Water and Sanitation Utilities (http://www.ib-net.org), which is administered by the World Bank, resulted in the inclusion of the large number of water utilities in the panel. The authors are particularly grateful to Alexander Danilenko for his help and support. Access to data was facilitated on several occasions by the intervention of a particular individual; among those to whom the authors owe thanks are Peter Thomson, Ignacio Iribarren, Valeriy Tsaplin, Yuriy Myroshnychenko, Rostyslav Goy, Xavier Cledan Mandri-Perrott, Jim Southworth, Anneli Ivanov, Edgar Saravia, Roman Palac, Adam Kuriata, and Ivan Ivanov. The authors also greatly appreciate the assistance received from the following regulators, investors, and utilities: the National Electricity Regulatory Commission of Ukraine, the Public Services Regulatory Commission of the Republic of Armenia, AES Corporation (United States), United Utilities (United Kingdom), Tallinna Vesi (Estonia), Eesti Energia AS (Estonia), Sofiyska Voda (Bulgaria), and Stoen (Poland).

Finally, various consultants gathered data in the field. The authors thank the following individuals for excellent work: Stephen Karekezi and the researchers associated with the African Energy Policy Research Network (Kenya); Valentin Arion (Moldova); Lenka Camrova (Czech Republic); Nazim Mammadov (Azerbaijan); Kis András (Hungary); Martin Rodriguez Pardina (Argentina); Guillermo Aber, Hugo Santa Maria, and Alvaro Quijandria (Peru); Alejandro Vivas (Colombia); Roberto M. Iglesias and Marina Figueira de Mello (Brazil); and Sergei Sivaev and Alexei Rodionov (Russian Federation). The following national and regional organizations participated in the fieldwork: the African Energy Policy Research Network (Kenya), the Water Utility Partnership for Capacity Building in Africa (Senegal), the Institute for Structural Policy (IREAS, Czech Republic), Apoyo Consultoria (Peru), the Institute for Urban Economics (Russian Federation), Macroconsulting (Argentina), and the Hungarian Environmental Economics Centre (MAKK, Hungary).

ABOUT THE AUTHORS

Katharina Gassner (kgassner@worldbank.org) is a senior economist in the Finance, Economics and Urban Department of the Sustainable Development Network of the World Bank. An expert in network regulation, she has worked in various areas relating to infrastructure, including policy and sector reform advice, public-private service delivery options, applied regulatory studies, and econometric research. She has developed standard guidelines for infrastructure assessment reports in energy and water, and has undertaken country studies in public finance and the cost of infrastructure service delivery to governments. Before joining the World Bank in 2003, Katharina worked for OXERA, a U.K.-based consulting firm specializing in network services. She holds a BS and an MS in economics from the University of Lausanne, an MS in politics of the world economy from the London School of Economics, and a PhD from the same institution.

Alexander Popov (Alexander.Popov@ecb.int) is a consultant for the Finance, Economics and Urban Department of the Sustainable Development Network of the World Bank. He undertook the econometric analysis featured in this study while a doctoral student in Chicago. After completing his PhD, Alexander joined the European Central Bank, where he works as a financial economist in the research department focusing on the effects of financial development and globalization on the real economy. He holds an MA in humanities from the University of Sofia and a PhD in economics from the University of Chicago.

Nataliya Pushak (npushak@worldbank.org) is a consultant for the Finance, Economics and Urban Department of the Sustainable Development Network of the World Bank. She has undertaken extensive quantitative research on infrastructure issues in developing countries and has contributed to studies of electricity tariff affordability and bill nonpayment, among others. She was part of a research team that developed and enhanced the PPIAF and World Bank's Private Participation in Infrastructure Project Database (http://ppi.worldbank.org/). Recently her research has focused on the role of investors from emerging economies. Her educational background includes a BA in economics from Lviv National University, an MA in sociology from the National University of Kyiv-Mohyla Academy, and an MPA in public finance from Indiana University.

ABBREVIATIONS

CAPEX	capital expenditures
FE	fixed effects
GDP	gross domestic product
GWh	gigawatt-hours
ITU	International Telecommunication Union
MWh	megawatt-hours
PPI	Private Participation in Infrastructure
PPIAF	Public-Private Infrastructure Advisory Facility
PSP	private sector participation
RE	random effects
SOE	state-owned enterprise
TT	time trend

OVERVIEW

Whether privately managed utilities outperform those run by the state is an old question. What makes it difficult to answer is that utilities such as water and electricity distribution companies do not operate in competitive markets, where a change from public to private management is expected to lead to cost savings and efficiency gains driven by the profit motive. Indeed, studies looking at privatized firms operating in competitive markets have reported increases in labor productivity, output, and investment and improvements in service quality.

The empirical results in electricity distribution and water and sanitation services are far less clear-cut. These services have features traditionally used to justify public involvement rather than characterizing a competitive market. They are natural monopolies (when the service is provided through networks), generate externalities, and are (particularly in the case of water services) considered a human right and an important element of social and development policies. The question of whether privately managed utilities outperform publicly run ones is especially difficult to answer in developing countries, where the effect of weak or inappropriate legal and institutional environments must also be taken into account.

Despite the obvious difficulties, understanding the tradeoffs between public and private management is critical for policy makers and their advisors. The private sector has long been advocated as a solution to closing the service delivery gap faced by developing countries. But the wide range of results observed case by case has led to strong feelings both for and against private involvement in utility services, and any resolution of the debate has often seemed far away.

The Study

To address the question as rigorously as possible and to distill universally applicable results from the multitude of evidence, this study examines the impact of private sector participation (PSP) in water and electricity distribution using a data set of more than 1,200 utilities in 71 developing and transition economies. The sample includes 301 utilities with PSP and 926 state-owned enterprises (SOEs) over more than a decade of operation. The data set compiled is unique in its coverage, and its size and composition make it possible to address for the first time methodological problems that have plagued empirical research and hampered conclusive results.

Studies on natural monopoly industries have traditionally suffered from small sample size and taken the form of case studies, which cannot produce generalizations. This study, by contrast, uses a database covering, as comprehensively as possible, all the electricity distribution and water and sanitation companies that experienced PSP between the beginning of the 1990s and 2002. Moreover, the study compares these PSP firms with a set of sufficiently similar state-owned utilities to establish meaningful—"like with like"—comparisons. Finally, because of the long period covered, the study is able to address the question of the counterfactual in a dynamic way, showing how the performance of firms with PSP changed over time and comparing that change with the performance of firms that remained state run.

Dual Estimation Strategy

To achieve robust results and isolate as much as possible the impact of introducing PSP from other external and internal changes that may also affect firms' performance, the study uses a dual estimation strategy. This dual approach controls for the fact that a utility is unlikely to be randomly selected for PSP and the possibility that the analysis might compare PSP cases with fundamentally dissimilar SOEs and thus produce biased results.

The study produces two sets of results: the first using a larger but potentially biased data set including all available SOEs as comparators; the second using a smaller set of SOEs carefully selected for their comparability. There is a tradeoff between the two approaches: the larger data set allows a richer differentiation of results by type of PSP and period, while the smaller one provides a more rigorous estimation, but at the cost of fewer observations and results. To ensure robust findings, the study reports only results confirmed by both models.

Differentiation by Contract Type

Much past research has concentrated on "pure privatization"—permanent private control over business assets and associated rights. But because of natural monopoly features and social and political considerations, full divestiture of assets is rare in electricity and especially so in water and sanitation. The study therefore examines the broad range of legal arrangements for involving the private sector—management and lease contracts, concessions, and partial as well as full divestitures—using the transfer of operating rights to determine whether a utility is privately operated.

The results are differentiated by type of contract. The strength of the PSP impact is expected to vary by contract type, and the predominant type differs by sector: divestitures (full and partial) account for most PSP cases in electricity distribution, and concessions account for most in water and sanitation.

The Results

The results of the study show that the private sector delivers on expectations of higher labor productivity and operational efficiency, convincingly outperforming a set of comparable companies that remained state owned and operated.

Performance Gains

Comparing average annual values for performance indicators from the pre- and post-PSP periods shows that PSP is associated with the following:

- A 12 percent increase in residential connections for water utilities
- A 54 percent increase in residential connections per worker for water utilities and a 29 percent increase for electricity distribution companies
- A 19 percent increase in residential coverage for sanitation services
- An 18 percent increase in water sold per worker (following the introduction of concession contracts) and a 32 percent increase in electricity sold per worker
- A 45 percent increase in bill collection rates in electricity
- An 11 percent reduction in distribution losses for electricity (following partial divestitures) and a 41 percent increase in the number of hours of daily water service.

All of these changes, occurring over a period of five years or more, are over and above those recorded for the state-owned companies.

Staff Reductions

The clear improvement in operational performance is encouraging for proponents of PSP. But the results also confirm one reason that introducing the private sector so often provokes fierce political resistance and public hostility: the labor productivity gains are linked to a reduction in staff numbers in both water and electricity (no separate results are available for sanitation), with the strongest effects for divestitures. Following the introduction of PSP, average employment falls by 24 percent in electricity and by 22 percent in water. In other words, on average, state-operated utilities use more employees than privately run ones to produce the same level of output.

Policy makers need to weigh the tradeoff between an increase in output and service quality and a reduction in staff. But it is worth bearing in mind that, while staff reductions are significant at the level of the utility, they occur over several years and are small relative to the national labor force. Moreover, the study considers all staff reductions—whether layoffs or natural attrition—to be the same.

No Clear Investment Gains

Proponents of PSP long hoped—and political leaders sometimes rashly promised—that greater private involvement in utility services would lead to vastly greater investment and thus to greater capacity and coverage. The study finds mixed evidence on this issue and so cannot conclude that investment always increases with PSP (despite the evidence of increases in water connections).

The investment question is best examined at a disaggregated level. For electricity divestitures, as economic theory predicts, investment per worker increases with PSP. For lease and management contracts, particularly relevant for water and sanitation, there is generally no investment obligation for the private party, and the results suggest that the public asset-holding company does not increase investment even if PSP brings operational improvements. For concession contracts there is no conclusive evidence that investment increases.

Investment data are notoriously difficult to measure, and the results need to be interpreted with care. Nevertheless, the evidence points to a lack of investment—public or private—in the maintenance and expansion of utility networks as a general rule, even where PSP leads to an increase in operational efficiency. This lack of investment raises concerns about the long-term sustainability of the operational improvements achieved.

No Systematic Change in Prices

A final key result relates to tariffs: except for electricity concessions, the study finds no evidence of a systematic change in residential prices as a result of PSP. Yet in developing countries, where below-cost pricing of essential utility services is well documented, higher tariffs for all but the poorest households are often recommended as part of reform, to give a utility enough resources to address shortfalls in service.

The lack of any substantial difference in tariffs between utilities with PSP and SOEs could have two explanations: tariffs changed in equal measure in both categories, or they did not change significantly in either of them. The second explanation seems more likely in countries where affordability is a real concern for much of the population. The result may point to the economic and political difficulties of aligning tariffs with the costs of service provision. Its implications for revenue streams call into question the sustainability of private involvement unless there are explicit subsidy payments. The result might also explain the lack of public or private investment.

The Question of Efficiency Gains

If the efficiency gains associated with the entry of a private operator do not translate into higher investment or lower prices, where do they go? One possible explanation is that services are initially so underpriced that even significant efficiency gains do not produce a financial equilibrium or justify lower prices. Instead, the efficiency gains translate into better operational performance, such as reductions in distribution losses, and the government spends less subsidizing its utilities.

Another explanation may be that the private operator reaps all the gains through profits. Given the young regulatory environments in developing countries, which often lack sufficient capacity for supervising public-private contracts, this possibility needs to be considered.

Conclusion

For each electricity or water utility that shifts from public to private operation, the potential for improving performance depends on a host of variables, observable and unobservable. No study can deal with every one of them in detail. Still, this study produces clear findings that the private sector delivers on operational performance and labor efficiency.

But the clear practical implications for labor mean that governments need to address the employment question seriously. Even though the observed staff reductions improve utilities' productivity and are small relative to national unemployment, measures to mitigate the effects should be put into place early on. The question is one of trading off the social costs of reform against the social costs of inaction.

The two other key findings relate to trends in investment and tariffs. Although the available data need to be further refined and analyzed, the study points to a worrying lack of investment in utilities by the public or private sector. And it finds no indication of tariffs moving closer to cost-recovery levels. These two findings are probably linked, and the subject deserves further attention from both researchers and reformers.

1.

INTRODUCTION

Whether privately managed utilities outperform those run by the state has long been debated. In competitive markets a change from public to private management is expected to lead to cost cutting and efficiency improvements driven by the profit motive, and when price exceeds marginal cost, a profit-driven operator will increase sales, thus benefiting consumers. This dynamic has traditionally been among the strongest arguments used by proponents of privatization.

Cost savings, improvements in service quality, and increases in labor productivity and investment have indeed been reported in competitive industries as a result of a shift from public to private ownership.[1] But the empirical results on the impact of private sector participation (PSP) in electricity distribution and water and sanitation services are less clear-cut. These utility services have features that have traditionally been used to justify public involvement: they are natural monopolies (when the service is provided through networks), they generate externalities, and, particularly in the case of water services, they display inelasticity of demand that conveys significant pricing power to the provider.[2] In the presence of such characteristics, economic research into the impact of private management has often been inconclusive.

[1] Gains in productivity and profitability associated with privatization have been demonstrated by, for example, Megginson, Nash, and van Randenborgh (1994); Frydman and others (1999); La Porta and López-de-Silanes (1999); Brown, Earle, and Telegdy (2006).

[2] See Galiani, Gertler, and Schargrodsky (2005) for a discussion of these elements in water services.

The interpretation of results is especially complex in developing and transition economies, which often have weak or inappropriate legal and institutional environments. Nevertheless, the wide-ranging introduction of PSP in electricity distribution and water and sanitation services in such economies in the past 25 years offers an opportunity to study its effect on enterprise performance in essential utility services. At the same time governments throughout the world have kept many utilities in state hands, providing a useful comparator group.

Previous studies of this issue have often provided inconclusive or ambiguous answers, in large part because of data limitations. First, studies on natural monopoly industries suffer from small sample size and often take the form of case studies, which cannot produce generalizations. Second, most studies look only at data from industrial countries and fail to assess how ownership and management models affect performance in weaker institutional environments. Third, many studies have analyzed the effect of private participation through a "before and after" comparison for a given set of companies; they have not observed the performance of comparators that remained state owned over the same period.[3] Finally, even where sufficient observations and a subsample of state-owned comparators are available,[4] the critical question of whether the control group of state-owned comparators can be considered a reliable counterfactual has been downplayed or ignored.

This study, using a data set and empirical approach designed to overcome those limitations, provides robust evidence that privately operated utilities surpass state-run utilities in operational performance and labor productivity.

Analytical Framework and Data

This study analyzes the effect of PSP on performance in electricity distribution and water and sanitation services using longer time series and more comprehensive coverage than previous research. The study also uses a set of state-owned comparators selected on the basis of two matching procedures—one less formal, the other more so—to avoid indiscriminate comparison of utilities that differ in many dimensions beyond private or public management, a comparison that can lead to biased results and misleading interpretation of data.

---

[3] For example, Galal and others (1994) and Boubakri and Cosset (1998) compare private companies before and after privatization without a sample of state-owned comparators.

[4] For example, Megginson, Nash, and van Randenborgh (1994); Brown, Earle, and Telegdy (2006).

The study developed a database that covers as well as possible the entire population of utilities that experienced private participation between the beginning of the 1990s and 2002. It covers the two sectors in all developing regions as defined by the World Bank: East Asia and Pacific, Europe and Central Asia, Latin America and the Caribbean, Middle East and North Africa, South Asia, and Sub-Saharan Africa. All PSP cases with at least three years of post-PSP experience were targeted for inclusion in the sample, resulting in an end date for the data collection of 2005. The question of the counterfactual was addressed by including in the database state-owned enterprises (SOEs) operating in the same sectors and countries or regions. The final sample consists of 301 utilities with PSP and 926 SOEs in 71 developing and transition economies.

By identifying utilities in a number of countries and following them over a number of years, the study created a data panel, a data set consisting of observations on a given number of firms observed over several periods. The final panel spans the years 1973–2005, although most of the data are concentrated in 1992–2004. Because the study rarely succeeded in securing a complete time series from 1992 to 2005 for a given utility, for either the PSP group or the SOE comparators, the panel should be viewed as unbalanced, an issue dealt with in the empirical strategy.

The study also improves on previous ones by covering a range of ways in which PSP has been introduced in water and electricity utilities. Much past research has examined "pure privatization": permanent private control over business assets and associated rights. But in electricity and water services, because of natural monopoly features and social and political considerations, full divestiture of assets occurs relatively rarely. Thus the study includes PSP experiences across the range of legal arrangements defining the role of the private sector: management and lease contracts, concessions, and partial and full divestitures.[5] The criterion used for determining whether a utility is privately operated is the transfer of operating rights.

[5] For the purposes of this study *full divestiture* is defined as the transfer of 100 percent of infrastructure assets, operating assets, and operating rights to private hands for an indefinite period; *partial divestiture* as the transfer of at least 51 percent but less than 100 percent of these assets and rights to private hands for an indefinite period; a *concession* as the transfer of these assets and rights for a limited period; a *lease contract* as state ownership of infrastructure assets, joint ownership of operating assets, and private ownership of operating rights for a limited period; and a *management contract* as state ownership of infrastructure and operating assets and private ownership of operating rights for a limited period. In addition, in a divestiture or concession, the private side earns the full revenue; in a lease contract, a percentage of the revenue; and in a management contract, a fixed or variable fee. For a detailed discussion of forms of PSP, see Delmon (2006).

Empirical Approach

The study uses several model specifications adapted to the characteristics of the data, starting with the least demanding random-effects specification and imposing an increasing number of control and correction mechanisms. The random-effects specification is most apt for the analysis of firms for which the study can be certain that there are no fixed "unobservables" over time, such as specific management, training, or work culture. The fixed-effects specification controls for such firm-specific effects, which are invariant over time but might be falsely interpreted as being the result of PSP. Finally, the model with firm-specific time trends controls for fixed effects among firms as well as different trend productivity growth rates that may affect the probability of a company having been chosen for PSP in the first place.

As an additional robustness check of the findings from the panel data, the study also uses a difference-in-differences estimation procedure with nearest-neighbor matching to choose the best subsample of SOE comparators from the full panel sample. The nearest-neighbor matching is based on a propensity score analysis applied to the utilities for which there is at least one observation before and one observation after the introduction of private participation. The procedure accounts for the data coverage problem in the data set: the fact that the panel is unbalanced and that pre-PSP data and post-PSP data are not observed equally for all utilities in the sample. That is, it corrects for the possibility that standard regression analysis overstates or understates the impact of PSP by comparing utilities that have PSP with state-owned utilities that were inferior or superior to begin with.

This combination of methods addresses the concerns traditionally raised about impact studies (see, for example, Ravallion 2001). The aim is to use the combined explanatory power of the two estimation strategies, each of which has advantages and drawbacks. The regression model using the full panel data makes the most of the uniquely extensive data set but suffers from an unbalanced panel and a potentially too dissimilar control group. The matching procedure corrects for these shortcomings but leads to a loss of data points and thus to less robustness and fewer results differentiated by contract type.

Transition Period and Contract Type

Similar to Andrẹs (2004), the study analyzes the dynamics of firm performance as a response to PSP in two periods: a transition period, encompassing the two years immediately before and the year after the entry of the private operator, and a post-PSP period, the period beginning at least one year after the private operator's entry. This procedure allows comparison of the effects of full private control of operating rights against possible anticipatory effects and the impact of restructuring of the utility immediately before private participation is introduced.[6] As in Andres (2004) and Brown, Earle, and Telegdy (2006), the study tries to isolate the "pure" effect of private participation from any transitory effect.

In addition, the study reports results on the range of effects observed for the different types of private participation most common in utility industries: full divestiture, partial divestiture, concession, and lease and management contracts. In the earlier literature the statistical differentiation of results by type of contract was hampered by small sample size. By contrast, this study includes a sufficient number of PSP contracts of different types. The two sectors examined show distinct patterns: in electricity distribution, full and partial divestitures clearly dominate; in water and sanitation services, concession contracts do.

Because different forms of PSP involve different contractual obligations, results would be expected to vary by type of contract. For example, lease and management contracts may have clauses explicitly limiting intervention by the private operator in labor decisions, while full divestitures give the private party much greater management control, a difference that could be expected to show up in different estimation results for these types of contracts. It can also be assumed that initial conditions drive the selection of performance targets for contracts. For example, long-term concession contracts with explicit expansion targets may be favored where increasing the number of residential connections is a primary policy objective, and here the data would be expected to reveal growth in connections. The variation in the panel allows examination of the link between type of contract and estimated impact of PSP.

Limitations and Caveats

Several limitations and caveats should be highlighted up front. First, the study undertakes a partial analysis only and does not attempt to assess economy-wide welfare effects of private sector entry. Moreover, the approach focuses on the supply side, and the results are interpreted accordingly. What is measured as a supply-side effect could well be at least partly demand driven; for example, an increase in output might be due to higher demand, not a change on the supply side.

Second, for clarity of argument the study uses a terminology opposing *utilities with PSP* to *state-owned enterprises*. This terminology implies a simpli-

[6] See also Brown, Earle, and Telegdy (2006) for a detailed discussion of timing effects and their econometric treatment.

fication of reality: for most of the PSP cases except full divestitures, state ownership of assets (if not operating rights) is still the rule. Moreover, the term SOEs is used in a broad sense, referring to utilities owned and controlled by government at all levels, whether central, provincial, or municipal.

Finally, the study does not explore the role of sector-specific and economy-wide institutional conditions and regulatory arrangements and how they influence the performance results. For example, it does not take into account the existence of a wider institutional reform program, the presence of a sector regulator, or the role of different tariff regulation regimes; doing so is recommended for further research.[7]

---

[7] See Gasmi, Noumba, and Virto (2006) for an exploration of the relationship among political institutions, regulation, and the effectiveness of reform in the case of telecommunications.

2.

EMPIRICAL LITERATURE

This study of the effect of private sector participation (PSP) on firm performance deals with two particular circumstances: it focuses on electricity and water distribution services, which are associated with natural monopoly characteristics, and on developing rather than industrial countries. The empirical literature spans a wide range of techniques and results relevant to this context.[1]

Techniques

The empirical techniques used to study the impact of private participation fall into three broad categories. The first, and arguably most straightforward, is analysis of the statistical significance of the difference in average values of performance indicators between state-owned enterprises (SOEs) and private companies (for example, Megginson, Nash, and van Randenborgh 1994; Boubakri and Cosset 1998; Hodge 1999). However, this technique suffers from an inability to control for determinants of performance other than the ownership variable and does not take into account differences in initial conditions between companies.

Thus a second set of studies attempt to isolate the effect of PSP over time, using panel data techniques (for example, Estache and Rossi 2002; Andres, Foster, and Guasch 2006; Brown, Earle, and Telegdy 2006). These studies correct for omitted-variable bias and consider initial conditions of companies. But they conduct a partial equilibrium analysis only; that is, they do not take into account general equilibrium considerations or welfare effects of PSP.

[1] See Briceño-Garmendia (2004) for a detailed survey of the literature in this setting.

These issues are addressed by a third set of studies that perform an empirical analysis with respect to a variety of economic agents affected (for example, Galal and others 1994; Chisari, Estache, and Romero 1999; Clarke, Ménard, and Zuluaga 2000; McKenzie and Mookherjee 2003; Galiani, Gertler, and Schargrodsky 2005).

Partial effects analyzed in the empirical literature on privatization include changes in several partial measures of performance: employment, output, and coverage (for example, Ramamurti 1996; Ros 1999; Ros and Banerjee 2000; Estache and Rossi 2002; Andres and others forthcoming) and degrees of efficiency and productivity (for example, productivity growth in Ehrlich and others 1994; labor productivity in Frydman and others 1999).

Findings

Most of the literature on the introduction of PSP in previously state-owned enterprises relates to manufacturing (for example, Vining and Boardman 1992; Frydman and others 1999; Brown, Earle, and Telegdy 2006). Multisector studies include Megginson, Nash, and van Randenborgh (1994), who treat no fewer than 32 different industries.

Among sectors traditionally counted as utility services, telecommunications has arguably received the most attention (for example, Ramamurti 1996; Ros 1999), followed by transport (for example, Ramamurti 1996; Laurin and Bozec 2001). In recent years several papers have made important empirical contributions on the electricity and water sectors. Some of the studies are based on case studies (for example, Galal and others 1994; La Porta and López-de-Silanes 1999), but others have produced more comprehensive cross-country analysis (such as Estache and Rossi 2002 and Andres, Foster, and Guasch 2006 for the electricity sector; Galiani, Gertler, and Schargrodsky 2005 for the water sector; Andres 2004 for water, electricity, and telecommunications).

Most studies on the impact of privatization focus on industrial countries (representative studies include Haskel and Szymanski 1993; Megginson, Nash, and van Randenborgh 1994). The reason for this imbalance, besides the fact that privatization programs were introduced earlier in industrial countries, is that data from developing countries have historically been insufficient. In the past couple of decades, however, as many nonindustrial countries have aggressively pursued privatization, the literature has been enriched by empirical analysis of the effect of private participation in developing countries, particularly in Latin America. Galal and others (1994) present case studies both for industrial countries and for developing ones; other studies have combined data from the two types of countries (for example, Megginson, Nash, and van Randenborgh 1994; Bortolotti and others 2001; Dewenter and Malatesta 2001).

All these studies find important increases in productivity, profitability, and access to services. Because of data aggregation, however, "mixed" studies suffer from heterogeneity problems with potentially misleading averaged results, an issue of concern in developing countries.

Studies focusing exclusively on developing countries have yielded interesting results. Boubakri and Cosset (1998), investigating the effect of the privatization of manufacturing firms in a sample of 21 developing countries in 1980–92, find significant improvements in profitability, operating efficiency, capital investment, output, and total employment. They show that these effects are larger in richer developing countries. Wallsten (2001), using data on telecommunications from 30 African and Latin American countries, finds that privatization is associated with greater access to services and lower prices, although only when privatization is coupled with an increase in competition and in the presence of independent regulation. Fink, Mattoo, and Rathindran (2002), using International Telecommunication Union (ITU) data for 86 developing countries in 1985–99, again find that the largest increases in quality appear when privatization is coupled with independent regulation. Finally, in a sample of Latin American countries, Andres (2004), Andres, Foster, and Guasch (2006), and Andres and others (forthcoming) find important increases in quality, investment, and labor productivity and a decrease in employment in telecommunications, electricity, and water distribution services.

Thus the empirical literature surveyed, for both industrial and developing countries, shows considerable support for a positive effect of private participation or ownership on efficiency, but there are enough ambiguous or contrary results to produce an inconclusive final picture.[2] In particular, the empirical studies on the effects of privatization or private participation over time in industrial and developing countries (for example, Ramamurti 1996; Ros 1999; Ros and Banerjee 2000; Estache and Rossi 2002; Andres, Foster, and Guasch 2006) all show that private participation is unambiguously associated with a decrease in the labor force, an increase in labor productivity, an increase in output, and an increase in coverage, efficiency, and quality of output (measured as, for example, a reduction in child mortality as a result of the

[2] Of the empirical papers surveyed in Briceño-Garmendia (2004), more than half show better results for firms with some kind of private participation, a third find ambiguous results, and the rest favor state ownership.

privatization of water distribution utilities in Galiani, Gertler, and Schargrodsky 2005).[3]

Among the studies that compare utilities with PSP to a sample of similar SOEs, trying to control for selection bias, some provide evidence of the effect of PSP on measures that this study does not cover, such as an increase in firm-level productivity growth (for example, Ehrlich and others 1994). Others find important effects on measures that this study does examine, such as an increase in efficiency and labor productivity (for example, Frydman and others 1999), although only for firms controlled by foreign owners. In an important departure from the other studies, Megginson, Nash, and van Randenborgh (1994) find a significant increase in the labor force as a result of privatization; this finding may well be linked to the fact that they examine manufacturing companies that pursue expansion strategies after improving efficiency. They also find a substantial increase in profitability, investment, and efficiency. Finally, Brown, Earle, and Telegdy (2006) find important increases in manufacturing total factor productivity in Hungary, Romania, and Ukraine in the post-1989 period.

The effect on the other measures on which this study focuses is less clear-cut. Ehrlich and others (1994) find a long-term decrease in total costs, while Frydman and others (1999) find no significant effect of a change in ownership on costs. And both Estache and Rossi (2002) and Andres, Foster, and Guasch (2006) find an ambiguous effect of privatization on prices. This result is along the lines of theoretical predictions, which point to two effects of PSP: a reduction in price due to an improvement in efficiency and an increase in price due to the elimination of explicit and implicit subsidies and cross-subsidies often present in the sectors analyzed. Which of these two effects will dominate depends on the initial situation and the regulatory environment.

[3] However, Wallsten (2001) finds no significant effect of change in ownership on coverage and labor efficiency when controlling for competition.

3.

SELECTION OF THE SAMPLE

Empirical analysis of private participation has traditionally suffered from selection bias. This problem arises when an independent variable is observed not for the entire population but only for a subset of the population. For example, a study might observe the price of electricity charged by the private sector participation (PSP) utilities once PSP has been introduced, but not observe it for similar utilities in which PSP has not been introduced. In such a setting it is possible to examine whether a variable has increased or decreased following PSP, but it is not possible to ascertain whether a similar change has occurred in the state owned companies.

Faced with this problem, this study determined a subsample of utilities with PSP and a corresponding subsample of state-owned utilities using qualitative criteria that ensure that the state-owned utilities are a valid counterfactual to PSP. The ideal would be to find pairs of PSP and state-owned utilities that operate in the same sector in the same country and that are otherwise sufficiently alike that any variation in performance could be closely linked to the variation in ownership. But the pool of available utilities in a country is by nature limited to very few (often a single one). Moreover, the available comparators often vary widely in such dimensions as size or customer base—factors that can influence company performance in the pre-PSP period, which may, in turn, affect post-PSP performance and bias the estimation.

Given the practical challenges of constructing the comparator sample, pragmatism and opportunism, along with a number of qualitative criteria, determined the initial state-owned enterprise (SOE) selection; as explained later, the most important minimum threshold for SOE candidates at the initial stage was that they had been corporatized. The resulting sample includes considerably more SOEs than PSP utilities, because the study deliberately "oversampled" SOEs to maximize the data for the econometric analysis. However, in a second step it then used finer estimation techniques that reduced the sample size but also ensured that utilities with PSP and those without were matched, as closely as possible, on the basis of pre-PSP characteristics. Results are reported for both the full sample and the smaller, closely matched sample because comparison of the two reveals the potential bias introduced by comparing SOEs and PSP companies indiscriminately.

Constructing a data panel by collecting data over a number of years for a number of utilities in different countries and regions, as this study does, makes it possible to compare the performance of the same utility before and after PSP is introduced as well as to compare PSP companies with state-owned comparators at a given point in time. Concretely, the study determines selection criteria that yield comparable samples of the PSP companies (the "treatment group") and the SOEs (the "control group"). For both treatment and control groups the study considers only utilities that distribute electricity or water to residential customers or provide sanitation services to households (that is, it excludes pure wholesale and industrial providers). For the PSP group it also considers only utilities for which information is available for at least three years after the entry of the private operator, to ensure enough data points to make the subsequent difference-in-differences estimation meaningful.

Treatment Group: Utilities with PSP

The aim for the treatment group is to represent as closely as possible the entire population of companies in the electricity distribution and water and sanitation sectors that experienced private participation between the beginning of the 1990s and 2002. The initial selection of PSP cases is based on the Public-Private Infrastructure Advisory Facility (PPIAF) and the World Bank's Private Participation in Infrastructure (PPI) Project Database.[1] From this starting point regional experts and consultants verified that all PSP cases in a given country and region were taken into account.

The selection process for the PSP sample is important because of the range of forms of private participation considered—from divestitures to management contracts. Determining whether a company truly belonged to the PSP sample was particularly important in sectors in which full divestiture rarely occurs, so that even after PSP is introduced the state normally retains some ownership of assets as well as a range of supervisory and control functions

[1] The PPI Project Database (http://ppi.worldbank.org) covers all low- and middle-income countries, as classified by the World Bank.

and powers. The study included in the PSP sample only the cases in which the private party has the power to make decisions that affect the firm's performance, such as those relating to output, inputs, technology, and service quality.

The determination of whether the private party exercises such managerial control turned out to be extremely utility specific, and no rule of thumb (such as private control of at least 50 percent of voting rights) proved to be always practicable. Indeed, for the initial list of PSP candidates the selection decision was greatly influenced not only by the type of PSP identified in the initial source of information, but also by the availability of reliable, nonconflicting information about the control mechanism in the utility and by the characteristics of the investor (or investors).[2] To overcome the lack of a standard rule for selection, the study analyzed each PSP candidate to determine whether it should indeed be included in the treatment group. Finally, to ensure the availability of post-PSP data, firms had to have been under private management for at least three years, resulting in a cutoff date for private entry of 2002.

The study covers, with at least partial data, 84 percent of the targeted PSP population, with 89 percent coverage in the electricity sector and 79 percent coverage in the water sector. Utilities for which a critical mass of data could not be gathered were excluded. It is assumed that this exclusion of targeted PSP companies from the final sample is randomized and thus does not introduce any bias.

For electricity the sample (of both PSP cases and SOEs) covers 448 million people across all regions considered. This represents coverage of only 21 percent of the population in the countries covered, however, and only 9 percent of the population in all regions.[3] The highest coverage rate is in Latin America and the Caribbean, where the sample covers 49 percent of the regional population. For water and sanitation the sample includes more utilities but covers less than half as many people as the electricity sample, 184 million. This represents coverage of 8 percent of the population in the countries covered and 4 percent of the entire population in all regions.

---

[2] No cooperatives are considered for the study. By their nature cooperatives are rarely, if ever, considered candidates for privatization, and they are excluded from both the PSP and the SOE group.

[3] The reason for the difference between the population in the countries covered and that in the regions covered is that not all countries in a region were included in the sample, because not all had a case of PSP or had been chosen for an SOE comparator. For each sector, the population share covered in each region and in each included country was derived by dividing the product of observed residential connections and average household size by total population (see Gassner, Popov, and Pushak 2008 for the data).

Control Group: State-Owned Utilities

One way to establish a control group is to examine the group of utilities selected for the treatment sample during the time when they were still under state control, for a "before and after" comparison. Because the analysis looks at the same firms, there are no concerns about lack of similarity between the two groups. The downside of this choice of comparator is that it assumes stationarity.

A second option takes stationarity into account by attempting to estimate the performance of the state company had it not been privatized and then comparing it with the performance of the firm with PSP. The study does not use this approach, judging the multiple assumptions required to estimate theoretical counterfactuals in a study of this size to be excessively hypothetical.

A third option, used by many privatization studies, is to select state companies in the same sector that have never been privatized and to construct a "with and without" comparison. Critics claim that this approach is not a true randomized experiment because the legal framework and policies under which state-owned firms operate differ from those applying to providers with PSP. Some of the differences might result in competitive advantages for the state-owned company (such as soft budget constraints, low or deferred taxes, and subsidized cost of capital); others might represent disadvantages (such as insufficient investment capital, mandatory social pricing, and interference in employment policies; see Shleifer 1998 for an extensive treatment). Despite these difficulties, the study selects the third option as the most practical solution to the control group aspect.

Ideally, the SOEs in the control group would operate as if they were privately owned and under a similar (ideally, identical) institutional framework so that any observed differences in performance could plausibly be attributed to ownership alone. That consideration leads to two questions. What factors other than operational control influence performance? And how can a control group be created that minimizes these factors? These questions lead to a set of criteria for inclusion in the control group.

The first criterion, as noted, is that the state company must have been corporatized; that is, the entity must be legally separate from the state, and its accounts must be separate and distinct from the government's. Corporatization also means operating with a clear commercial objective and under a commercial law framework—that is, being incorporated under general corporate law even if the precise relationship between the state as owner and the corporation (SOE) is set out in specific legislation or regulations. (This is the position in which SOEs usually find themselves after undergoing some kind of restructuring or while being prepared for privatization.)

One might next make a randomized selection from the comprehensive list of qualifying candidates for the control group—that is, all state-owned, corporatized water and electricity distribution companies in the countries and regions covered by the study. This approach would produce an impractically large number of SOEs. More important, it would not control for the many other characteristics in which the treatment and control groups differ, such as political and legal climate, country wealth, or size and activity area of the utility.

Therefore, once the PSP sample is identified, the first step is to consider SOEs in the same country as first candidates for the control group. If the country with a PSP company has no appropriate state counterpart, criteria are specified for countries that can be considered reasonable candidates for substitution. Countries that are nearby and have a similar economic and political environment are first choices. Cultural characteristics might also be important (for example, in some countries low bill-collection rates are common for historical reasons). The practical variables eventually chosen are gross domestic product (GDP) per capita, to ensure a similar stage of development and similar purchasing power of households; geographic proximity, as a proxy for regional characteristics; and features of market structure (for example, unbundling or not) and adopted reform framework. In summary, the strategy used to select the initial SOE control group was as follows:

- First, similar SOEs in the same country, same sector, run as if private
- Second, similar SOEs in the same country, same sector, marked for privatization
- Third, similar SOEs in a different but similar country, same sector, run as if private
- Fourth, similar SOEs in a different but similar country, same sector, marked for privatization
- Fifth, similar SOEs in the same country, same sector, not run as if private
- Sixth, similar SOEs in a different but similar country, same sector, not run as if private.

As always, the availability and quality of the utility-level data influenced the final selection. Most of the data come directly from the utilities or from regulatory agencies, existing national and World Bank utility databases, and academic and consultant studies.

Final Sample

The final sample of utilities includes 250 electricity companies in 53 countries and 977 water utilities in 48 countries (see figure 3.1). Altogether, the study uses data on 1,227 companies from 71 countries, spanning the years from 1973 to 2005 (see appendix A).

Electricity Sample

For electricity the study examines 160 companies under effective private management control and 90 SOE counterparts. Recall that the PSP sample is intended to represent the total population of companies with private involvement in a region. Latin America and the Caribbean has the largest number of privately operated utilities in electricity distribution, followed by Europe and Central Asia. The other regions have few cases with qualifying private participation. Consequently, 69 percent of the PSP sample for electricity comes from Latin America and the Caribbean, 22 percent comes from Europe and Central Asia, and the other regions are represented only marginally (see table 3.1).

Because of the pervasiveness of PSP in electricity distribution in Latin America, however, there is a shortage of comparable SOEs to match all the selected PSP cases in the region. Thus, although outside Latin America the numbers of PSP cases and SOEs in electricity are relatively well balanced, within that region there are considerably more PSP cases than SOEs. Still, the

Figure 3.1 Sample of PSP Cases and SOEs, by Sector

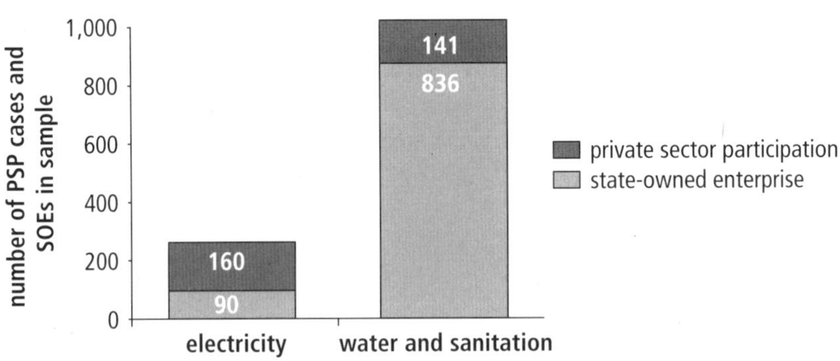

Source: Authors' calculations.

Table 3.1 Electricity Sample, by Region

Region	PSP		SOE		Total	
	Number	Percent of PSP sample	Number	Percent of SOE sample	Number	Percent of total
Latin America and the Caribbean	111	69	44	49	155	62
Europe and Central Asia	35	22	21	23	56	22
Sub-Saharan Africa	9	6	18	20	27	11
South Asia	3	2	3	3	6	2
East Asia and Pacific	1	1	2	2	3	1
Middle East and North Africa	1	1	2	2	3	1
Total	160	100	90	100	250	100

Source: Authors' calculations.

study has collected substantial SOE data, with the greatest share of SOEs (49 percent) still coming from Latin America.

Divestitures, both full and partial, make up 90 percent of the PSP sample for electricity (see figure 3.2). Concession contracts account for 9 percent. In this sample at least, lease and management contracts are the least popular contractual arrangements chosen for private involvement in electricity distribution, with only three instances recorded.

Water and Sanitation Sample

In the water and sanitation sample SOEs outnumber PSP cases in all regions. The overall sample consists of 977 utilities: 141 PSP utilities and 836 SOEs. In addition to initially targeted SOE counterparts, the sample includes all extra SOE data available in existing databases, greatly enhancing the ability to test the robustness of the results. While water supply and sanitation services are mostly supplied by integrated companies, separate analysis of the two services is made possible by the collection of indicators specific to each (see appendix A).

Latin America and the Caribbean again has the largest number of PSP cases, with almost 67 percent of the PSP sample for water and sanitation (see table 3.2). Europe and Central Asia accounts for 21 percent, East Asia and Pacific accounts for 7 percent, and the Middle East and North Africa and

Figure 3.2 Sample of PSP Cases for Electricity, by Type of Contract

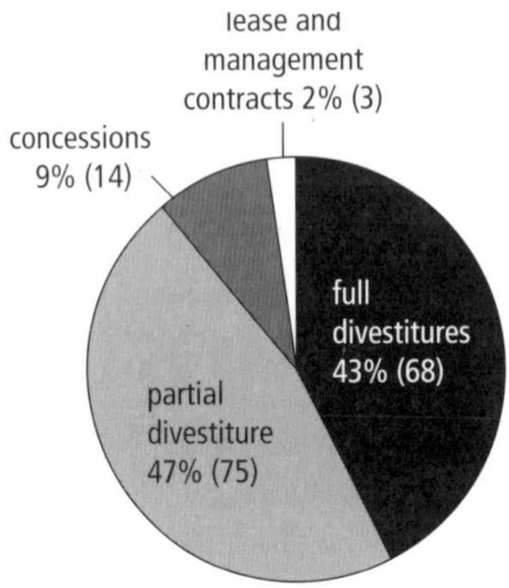

Source: Authors' calculations.
Note: Figures in parentheses are number of cases.

Figure 3.3 Sample of PSP Cases for Water and Sanitation, by Type of Contract

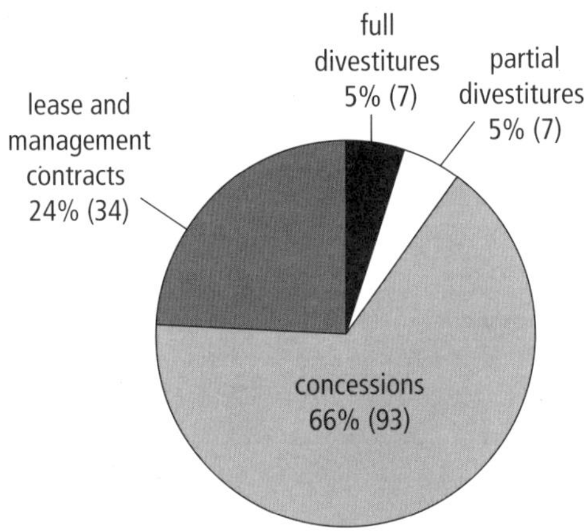

Source: Authors' calculations.
Note: Figures in parentheses are number of cases.

Table 3.2 Water and Sanitation Sample, by Region

Region	PSP		SOE		Total	
	Number	Percent of PSP sample	Number	Percent of SOE sample	Number	Percent of total
Latin America and the Caribbean	94	67	330	39	424	43
Europe and Central Asia	29	21	365	44	394	40
East Asia and Pacific	10	7	87	10	97	10
Middle East and North Africa	4	3	29	3	33	3
Sub-Saharan Africa	4	3	25	3	29	3
South Asia	0	0	0	0	0	0
Total	141	100	836	100	977	100

Source: Authors' calculations.

Sub-Saharan Africa account for 3 percent each. South Asia had no qualifying PSP cases at the time of data collection.

Unlike in electricity distribution, in water and sanitation divestiture has been tried in only a small number of utilities. Instead, operational control is transferred to private operators, while ownership of the assets remains with the state. One reason for the lack of divestitures in the water sector may be that selling public water assets to the private sector is politically sensitive. Another is that water is particularly underpriced relative to the marginal cost of supply; investors may well be aware of this and therefore be reluctant to take on the full risk of ownership, given the historic reluctance of governments to pay or to allow cost-recovery tariffs. Historically, the model for PSP in the water sector has been contracts providing for less than full ownership, exemplified by the French approach of concession and affermage contracts.

Accordingly, concession contracts account for 66 percent of the PSP sample for water and sanitation, management contracts account for 20 percent, and lease contracts account for 4 percent. Divestitures, full and partial, make up only 10 percent of the sample (see figure 3.3).

4.

EMPIRICAL METHODOLOGY

This study follows the broader literature on the impact of private ownership in estimating reduced-form equations for firm-level output, employment, labor productivity, price, coverage, and service quality, while accounting for unobserved heterogeneity and selection bias. Two main strategies have emerged for estimating the effect of introducing private management. Megginson, Nash, and van Randenborgh (1994) give rise to the first strategy, which uses differences in means and medians between the PSP and SOE samples and then tests the statistical significance of those differences. This methodology can be used to estimate differences in distribution either between private and state-owned firms observed during the same period or between private firms observed before and after privatization.

The second strategy stems from the treatment literature (notably, Heckman and Robb 1986). It uses a dummy variable equal to 1 for the postprivatization period and then tests the statistical significance of the coefficient on the dummy variable as well as that of different interaction terms that include the dummy variable. A variation of the technique explicitly takes transition effects into account by adding to the specification a second dummy variable equal to 1 for the period immediately before and after the entry of the private party (for example, Andres 2004; Andres, Foster, and Guasch 2006; Brown, Earle, and Telegdy 2006). In the context of a panel most impact studies use a difference-in-differences technique to account simultaneously for the difference between periods before and after an event and for that between treatment and control groups (see Ravallion 2001 for a discussion).

Overview of Empirical Analysis

The first, nonstructural strategy is particularly helpful when there are data for too few years to carry out a full-fledged panel data analysis. This study, because its panel spans a large number of years, focuses on the second, structural strategy to make the most of the rich information at its disposal. The regression-based strategy also makes it possible to account for bias caused by the endogeneity of the private sector participation (PSP) decision; the study addresses this issue by controlling for utility fixed effects and utility random growth and by using an instrumental variable procedure for the choice of PSP and for the type of contractual arrangement selected.

While the panel is very large overall, it is nevertheless unbalanced. Data gaps, particularly for the pre-PSP period, are problematic to the extent to which, for example, high labor productivity for a utility with PSP, observed in the post-PSP period only, may lead to an overestimation of the effect of PSP as a result of the study's not observing the utility's (potentially even higher) labor productivity in the pre-PSP period. In addition, the "unscientific" sampling of state-owned enterprises (SOEs) may result in the study comparing utilities that already differed on the basis of pre-PSP attributes; in other words, because of the opportunistic oversampling, the study may end up with a control sample that is too different from the treatment group to yield valid estimates.

To correct for the panel imbalances, the study performs a difference-in-differences estimation on the subset of companies for which there is at least one pre- and one post-PSP observation and then enhances the analysis with nearest-neighbor matching based on propensity scores. This is in the spirit of, for example, Card and Krueger (1993). The nearest-neighbor matching is used as a robustness check for the panel estimates calculated with the full sample; coefficients statistically significant in all approaches have a very high degree of confidence for assessing the impact of PSP.

To summarize, the empirical analysis proceeds in several steps. First, it undertakes a structural estimation of the difference between the treatment and control groups by performing a regression on the full panel with several specifications. Second, it eliminates the destabilizing factor of working with an unbalanced panel by reducing the sample to one in which all remaining utilities have at least one pre- and one post-PSP observation. Third, it accounts for the possibility that the decision to privatize was not random and that the PSP and SOE samples were different to start with. This would imply that the estimation results are biased, and the analysis addresses this by using a matching procedure. To do this, the analysis chooses the best comparators by using propensity score nearest-neighbor matching on the sample of companies with pre-PSP data.

Panel Data Analysis

In the first step, testing the significance of the dummy variable denoting PSP occurrence, the analysis also attempts to distinguish between effects of pure PSP and effects that arose during the years immediately before the transfer of control, when the government might restructure the utility to make it more attractive to private investors, and the year immediately after the transfer, when one-off changes in management occurred (see Brown, Earle, and Telegdy 2006 for a discussion of this phenomenon). The basic model estimated for each sector can be specified as a two-way linear regression model:

$$y_{ijt} = \beta_{PRIV} D_{ijt}^{PRIV} + \beta_{TRANS} D_{ijt}^{TRANS} + \delta_i \varphi_i + u_{ijt}, \tag{4.1}$$

where y_{ijt} is the natural logarithm of the variable of interest for firm i in country j at time t; D_{ijt}^{TRANS} is a dummy variable equal to 1 if the utility is a PSP observed during the transition period, $-2 \leq t \leq 1$, where $t = 0$ is the year of introduction of PSP; and u_{ijt} is the idiosyncratic error. The estimation is performed on the full panel.

The dimensions of the other variables vary across specifications and tests. In particular, the analysis uses two basic specifications related to the form of PSP: the first makes no distinction among different types of PSP contracts; the second one does. D_{ijt}^{PRIV} is the measure related to the type of contract. In the specification in which PSP contracts are aggregated, it is a dummy variable equal to 1 if firm i in country j has private participation at time t $\geq$ 2, where $t = 0$ is the year of introduction of PSP. By contrast, in the specification in which PSP contracts are disaggregated, D_{ijt}^{PRIV} is an $IT \times 4$ matrix composed of the four $IT \times 1$ vectors, $D_{ijt}^{FullDivest}$, $D_{ijt}^{PartialDivest}$, $D_{ijt}^{Concession}$, and $D_{ijt}^{LeaseMan}$, where the ijt element of $D_{ijt}^{FullDivest}$ is equal to 1 if the utility is a full divestiture at time t $\geq$ 2 and equal to 0 otherwise, the ijt element of $D_{ijt}^{PartialDivest}$ is equal to 1 if the utility is a partial divestiture at time t $\geq$ 2 and equal to 0 otherwise, the ijt element of $D_{ijt}^{Concession}$ is equal to 1 if the utility is a concession at time $t \geq 2$ and equal to 0 otherwise, and the ijt element of $D_{ijt}^{LeaseMan}$ is equal to 1 if the utility is under a lease or management contract at time $t \geq 2$ and equal to 0 otherwise.[1]

For $\delta_i \varphi_t$, the analysis tests three specifications. In the random-effects (RE) model $\varphi_t = 0$. In the fixed-effects (FE) model $\varphi_t = 1$, and consequently δ_i is the unobserved utility fixed effect. And in the fixed-effects with time trend (FE + TT) model $\varphi_t = (1, t)$ and consequently, $\delta_i = (\delta_i^1, \delta_i^2)$, where δ_i^1 is the unob-

[1] Lease and management contracts are aggregated because there are too few observations for each separately. This implies a need to assume that the two types of contracts do not differ much in the strength of the incentives they offer to the private operator.

served utility fixed effect and δ_i^2 is the utility-level random trend for utility i. The time trend is included to correct for the fact that some of the observed effects may be biased as a result of a natural demand-driven increase as the population grows, as well as to pick up some pre-PSP selection considerations.

Because the model used in the panel data analysis implies a semilogarithmic relationship between the dummy variables and the variables of interest in levels, the percentage impact of the change in value of the dummy variable from 0 to 1 is given by $e^{\beta PRIV} - 1$ and $e^{\beta TRANS} - 1$ (Halvorsen and Palmquist 1980). For example, $\beta_{PRIV} = 1$ would imply an increase in the value of the dependent variable by 172 percentage points from the pre-PSP to the post-PSP period. In addition, a generalized least squares specification is needed to correct for possible nonspherical errors. Because the true variance-covariance matrix is unknown, the analysis replaces it with a consistent estimator using the sample residuals, essentially employing a feasible generalized least squares procedure to estimate equation 4.1 in its different specifications.

Difference-in-Differences Estimation

Next the analysis uses Heckman and Robb's (1986) methodology to calculate difference-in-differences estimates enhanced by the use of a nearest-neighbor matching technique and thus to improve the robustness of the results. The rationale behind the dual strategy is twofold. First, as pointed out, the panel is unbalanced, and there are post-PSP observations for utilities with no corresponding pre-PSP data points. Thus while these observations are included in the panel specifications so as not to lose information, the PSP effects estimated through a regular panel procedure may be contaminated by an inability to determine whether the observed post-PSP value for a utility is an increase or a decrease relative to the pre-PSP period.

Second, even if the utilities with missing pre-PSP observations are dropped, using all SOEs indiscriminately in the comparator sample may result in an underestimation or an overestimation of the impact of PSP because of systematic ex-ante differences between the PSP and SOE samples. Comparing measures of labor productivity for PSPs that are on average large with those for SOEs that are on average small, for example, will introduce a bias in the estimation. These issues are addressed through a nearest-neighbor matching procedure in which utilities with PSP are matched with state-owned utilities on the basis of pre-PSP propensity score analysis. Using difference-in-differences specification with matching reduces the sample size, but it improves the robustness of the results by explicitly accounting for the concerns raised by the unbalanced sample and selection bias.

The following equation is estimated:

$$y_{ijt} = \beta_{PRIV} D_{ijt}^{PRIV} + \beta_{TREATMENT} D_{ijt}^{TREATMENT} + \beta_3 D_{ijt}^{PRIV} D_{ijt}^{TREATMENT} + u_{ijt}, \qquad (4.2)$$

where $t = 1, 2$, D_{ijt}^{PRIV} is a dummy variable equal to 1 if utility i in country j is observed post-PSP at time t = 2, and $D_{ijt}^{TREATMENT}$ is a dummy variable equal to 1 if utility i in country j is a PSP utility.

Thus for each utility the available yearly observations are averaged into two observations, one pre- and one post-PSP, where for state-owned utilities the "PSP year" is defined as the average year PSP was introduced in the country or, if there are no PSP cases in the country, in the region. A propensity score analysis is undertaken on the basis of the variables identified as significant in the choice of PSP, and state-owned utilities are assigned in a nearest-neighbor matching procedure to utilities with PSP. The procedure ensures that only the most closely matched SOEs act as the control group. Finally, a difference-in-differences analysis as specified in equation 4.2 is performed on the sample of matched utilities. The variable of interest here is the difference-in-differences estimator β_3, which gives the effect of PSP for a utility that is in the treatment group and is observed post-PSP.

To identify the variables significant in the choice of PSP—that is, what pre-PSP criteria can best predict the probability that a utility will be selected for PSP in the future—the study estimates a Cox proportionate hazard model of the probability of transition from full state control to some form of PSP (see appendix C). The variables whose coefficients are significant in this procedure are those used to calculate the propensity scores for matching companies, notably pre-PSP numbers of customers or staff and country-level variables such as gross domestic product (GDP) per capita, inflation, and unemployment rates.

For both the electricity and the water sector the results of the Cox model estimation show that utilities with more residential connections are more likely to be chosen for PSP. Unemployment, GDP per capita, and inflation in the pre-PSP period also appear to influence the probability of PSP in both sectors, although the direction of the effect is not necessarily the same in the two sectors.

This is an important outcome: the estimates suggest that governments do not introduce PSP randomly in water and electricity distribution. Moreover, the estimation results justify the use of propensity score matching: using a nearest-neighbor matching procedure to match utilities with PSP to state-owned utilities that are similar across the range of utility-level characteristics identified by the Cox proportionate hazard estimates will correct for bias in the results for PSP impact that are caused by pre-PSP characteristics.

5.

EMPIRICAL RESULTS

Key results from two different estimation approaches suggest that private sector participation (PSP) has a strong effect (see table 5.1). But the changes occur over the period 1992–2005, not as a sudden shift following the introduction of private management. For example, the 20–25 percent decrease in employment in water and electricity is an average change between the pre-PSP and the post-PSP period for utilities with PSP, over and above the change for state-owned utilities, and it occurs over multiple years.

Table 5.1 reports only selected results chosen because of their strength across all specifications of the two estimation approaches or their significance for interpretation. To allow closer examination of the difference between the two estimation approaches and the robustness of the results across different types of PSP, table 5.2 gives a complete picture of the impact variables analyzed. The table illustrates the important fact that the estimation results do not necessarily remain stable; it is also important to keep in mind that the difference-in-differences approach with matching leads to an important reduction in observation points and thus to fewer results.

For investment (CAPEX, capital expenditures) per worker, for example, PSP is observed to have some positive effect in the electricity sample that includes all state-owned enterprises (SOEs). But there are not enough data to confirm this effect when SOEs and PSP utilities are matched on the basis of pre-PSP characteristics. This leads us to conclude that there is no significant difference between privately and publicly managed utilities in this respect when pre-PSP characteristics are taken into account.

Table 5.1 Effect of PSP on Performance: Selected Results

Change in impact variable implied by regression coefficient (%)			
	Regression on full panel[a]		
Impact variable	Post-PSP	Transition	Difference-in-differences with matching post-PSP[b]
Electricity			
Employees	-24 ⇓***	-5 ⇓**	-28 ⇓***
Electricity sold per worker	32 ⇑***	1 ⇔	50 ⇑***
Residential connections per worker	29 ⇑***	4 ⇔	42 ⇑***
Collection rate	45 ⇑***	20 ⇑***	63 ⇑**
Electricity lost in distribution[c]	-11 ⇓***	11 ⇑***	−14 ⇓*
CAPEX per worker	54 ⇑*	34 ⇔	—
Average residential tariff	1.2 ⇔	6 ⇑*	−11 ⇔
Water			
Residential connections	12 ⇑***	8 ⇑***	38 ⇑*
Employees	−22 ⇓***	−12 ⇓***	2 ⇔
Water sold per worker[d]	18 ⇑*	6 ⇔	154 ⇑***
Residential connections per worker	54 ⇑***	28 ⇑***	151 ⇑***
Water lost in distribution	−23 ⇓***	−8 ⇔	−8 ⇔
Hours with water daily	41 ⇑***	15 ⇑***	12 ⇔
Average residential tariff	0 ⇔	4 ⇔	−2 ⇔

Sanitation						
Residential connections per worker	37	⇑***	19	⇑**	—	
Residential coverage	19	⇑***	18	⇑***	5	⇔

Source: Authors' calculations.

Note: ⇑ denotes a statistically significant increase associated with PSP, ⇓ denotes a statistically significant decrease, ⇔ denotes an ambiguous or not statistically significant result, — = insufficient data are available.

a. Numeric values in the post-PSP column should be read as the average change from the pre-PSP to the post-PSP period for utilities with PSP, over and above the change for state-owned utilities for the same period, and spanning a number of years. Transition refers to the transition period immediately before and after the introduction of PSP. The specification reported is the panel regression with fixed effects for utility, country, and year and firm-specific time trend for the full sample.

b. Difference-in-differences estimator, with nearest-neighbor matching undertaken to select the most comparable SOE counterparts. The sample is reduced to utilities with at least one pre- and one post-PSP observation.

c. Result applies to the specific case of partial divestitures.

d. Result applies to the specific case of concession contracts.

* Significant at 10 percent level.

** Significant at 5 percent level.

*** Significant at 1 percent level.

Table 5.2 Effect of PSP on Performance: Results for All Impact Variables

Change in impact variable implied by regression coefficient (%)								
					Regression on full panel (FE + TT)[a]			
Impact variable	**Post-PSP**		**Post-DF**		**Post-DP**		**Post-Cons**	
Electricity								
Residential connections	2.4	⇑*	−2.8	⇔	0.03	⇑*	21.3	⇑***
Electricity sold per connection	2.8	⇑*	15.6	⇑***	−1.8	⇔	1.2	⇔
Employees	−24.0	⇓***	−27.2	⇓***	−25.1	⇓***	12.1	⇔
Electricity sold per worker	31.5	⇑***	37.6	⇑***	32.6	⇑***	−3.5	⇔
Residential connections per worker	28.7	⇑***	29.7	⇑***	32.4	⇑***	−21.8	⇓**
Residential coverage[c]	−8.9	⇓***	−9.5	⇓***	—		−7.7	⇓*
Collection rate	45.4	⇑***	42.8	⇑***	67.5	⇑***	39.9	⇑***
Electricity lost in distribution	−12.6	⇓***	−17.2	⇓***	−11.0	⇓***	−10.4	⇔
Annual supply interruptions	9.6	⇔	−6.6	⇔	4.9	⇔	85.0	⇑***
CAPEX per worker	53.6	⇑*	31.1	⇔	88.5	⇑**	66.9	⇔
Average residential tariff	1.2	⇔	0.8	⇔	−1.0	⇔	35.0	⇑***
Water								
Residential connections	12.4	⇑***	17.4	⇑***	−0.6	⇔	14.7	⇑***
Water sold per connection	22.8	⇑**	0.0		−23.7	⇔	30.7	⇑***
Employees	−22.1	⇓***	−21.4	⇓***	−34.0	⇓***	−20.0	⇓***
Water sold per worker	27.0	⇑***	—		62.3	⇑*	18.4	⇑*
Residential connections per worker	53.7	⇑**	53.9	⇑***	77.5	⇑***	47.0	⇑***
Residential coverage	−6.3	⇓***	−14.4	⇓***	−12.5	⇑***	−2.2	⇔
Collection rate	3.3	⇔	—		1.1	⇔	3.6	⇔
Water lost in distribution	−22.9	⇓***	—		−27.8	⇔	−24.3	⇓***
Hours with water daily	40.6	⇑***	—		19.4	⇔	38.3	⇑***
CAPEX per worker	94.4	⇔	—		182.9	⇔	59.5	⇔
Average residential tariff	0.1	⇔	−2.3	⇔	−0.1	⇔	−2.7	⇔
Sanitation								
Residential connections	0.8	⇔	5.3	⇔	1.1	⇔	−2.1	⇔
Wastewater treated per connection	−21.3	⇔	—		−27.2	⇔	−17.8	⇔
Wastewater treated per worker	32.8	⇑**	—		108.3	⇑***	11.0	⇔
Residential connections per worker	36.8	⇑***	33.0	⇑*	58.9	⇑***	27.0	⇑***
Residential coverage	19.4	⇑***	39.7	⇑***	8.4	⇔	21.9	⇔***
Sewerage blockages per connection	73.7	⇔	—		—		138.9	⇔

		Difference-in-differences with matching[b]				
Post-L&M	Transition	Post-PSP	Post-DF	Post-DP	Post-Cons	Post-L&M
10.8 ⇔	0.9 ⇔	2.5 ⇔	−3.9 ⇑	12.4 ⇑**	12.9 ⇔	—
−2.4 ⇔	−2.3 ⇓*	−1.5 ⇔	16.9 ⇔	0.3 ⇔	−21.2 ⇔	—
2.3 ⇔	−4.6 ⇓**	−28.3 ⇓***	−47.1 ⇓***	−14.5 ⇔	2.3 ⇔	—
—	0.9 ⇔	50.2 ⇑***	134.1 ⇑**	23.0 ⇔	−39.0 ⇓***	—
—	3.8 ⇔	41.5 ⇑***	97.2 ⇑***	20.3 ⇔	−9.6 ⇔	—
—	−7.8 ⇓***	—	—	—	—	—
24.1 ⇔	19.5 ⇑***	63.2 ⇑**	—	—	—	—
36.6 ⇔	10.6 ⇑***	−8.9 ⇔	−6.3 ⇔	−14.3 ⇓*	−12.5 ⇔	—
—	38.5 ⇑***	−10.0 ⇔	—	−28.3 ⇓*	—	—
−71.1 ⇔	34.2 ⇔	—	—	—	—	—
—	5.7 ⇑*	−10.7 ⇔	15.9 ⇔	−7.2 ⇔	—	—
19.4 ⇑***	7.8 ⇑***	38.3 ⇑*	—	40.4 ⇔	44.0 ⇑*	—
14.2 ⇔	8.1 ⇔	16.6 ⇔	—	—	−4.1 ⇔	10.0 ⇔
−21.4 ⇓***	−12.3 ⇓***	2.0 ⇔	−35.5 ⇓***	−44.5 ⇓***	8.6 ⇔	−0.1 ⇔
40.1 ⇑***	5.8 ⇔	19.9 ⇔	—	—	153.9 ⇑***	29.4 ⇔
51.1 ⇑***	28.3 ⇑***	151.3 ⇑***	—	84.9 ⇑***	49.6 ⇔	—
−11.1 ⇓***	−7.0 ⇓***	−8.0 ⇔	—	−4.7 ⇔	30.9 ⇑**	−54.1 ⇔
1.3 ⇔	0.9 ⇔	3.8 ⇔	—	—	3.8 ⇔	—
−19.6 ⇓**	−8.1 ⇔	−8.2 ⇔	—	—	−36.3 ⇔	38.7 ⇔
48.6 ⇑***	14.8 ⇑***	11.6 ⇔	—	—	—	20.1 ⇔
326.3 ⇔	34.0 ⇔	—	—	—	—	—
10.4 ⇔	3.8 ⇔	−2.3 ⇔	—	—	4.3 ⇔	—
7.7 ⇔	4.3 ⇔	—	—	−35.4 ⇔	—	—
−40.6 ⇔	−19.3 ⇔	—	—	—	—	—
—	0.4 ⇔	—	—	—	—	—
42.0 ⇑***	19.1 ⇑**	—	—	—	—	—
19.8 ⇑***	17.7 ⇑***	4.5 ⇔	—	—	19.1 ⇔	−10.7 ⇔
22.6 ⇔	−10.8 ⇔	—	—	—	—	—

continued

Table 5.2 Effect of PSP on Performance: Results for All Impact Variables *(Continued)*

Source: Authors' calculations.
Note: ⇑ denotes a statistically significant increase associated with PSP, ⇓ denotes a statistically significant decrease, and ⇔ denotes an ambiguous or not statistically significant result. DF = full divestitures; DP = partial divestitures; Cons = concession contracts; L&M = lease and management contracts; CAPEX = capital expenditures; — = insufficient data are available.
a. Numeric values in the post-PSP column should be read as the average change from the pre-PSP to the post-PSP period for utilities with PSP, over and above the change for state-owned utilities for the same period, and spanning a number of years. Transition refers to the transition period immediately before and after the introduction of PSP. The specification reported is the panel regression with fixed effects for utility, country, and year and firm-specific time trend for the full sample.
b. Difference-in-differences estimator, with nearest-neighbor matching undertaken to select the most comparable SOE counterparts. The sample is reduced to utilities with at least one pre- and one post-PSP observation.
c. The quality of the coverage data for electricity was judged too unreliable for meaningful interpretation.
* Significant at 10 percent level.
** Significant at 5 percent level.
*** Significant at 1 percent level.

This example also illustrates why combining the two approaches is important: while the matching procedure does not support the result that investment per worker increases, this correction mechanism eliminates all but a handful of companies from the sample. The lack of a conclusive result from the matching procedure thus needs to be weighed against the loss of comprehensive data.[1]

The main message is twofold. First, the changes in results due to nearest-neighbor matching suggest that previous studies on privatization and PSP may have misestimated the effect of the shift from public to private control by comparing indiscriminately utilities with PSP and those without and by not taking into account ex-ante differences in the utilities chosen for PSP. Second, the study's main conclusion becomes even stronger when the complexity of the evidence is considered: across different model specifications and after a series of correction mechanisms, the study finds robust evidence in the global sample that PSP has a strong impact on performance and quality of service.

The results reported in the following sections, from the fixed effects with time trend (FE + TT) model (full sample) and the difference-in-differences model with propensity score matching, are those that survive all data manipulation and econometric techniques and thus have a high level of reliability. (See the tables in appendix D for the complete estimation results from these

[1] Because of the loss of observations, the matching procedure does not support the estimation of effects during the transition period.

two models as well as those from the random-effects model and the difference-in-differences model without propensity score matching.)

Electricity

For electricity some of the most striking results from the full panel estimation—confirmed by robust results in the difference-in-differences estimations—are those showing that PSP is associated with an increase in electricity sold per worker of 32 percent, an increase in the bill collection rate of 45 percent, and a reduction in distribution losses of 11 percent[2]—all over and above the change for state-owned utilities during the same period. The evidence also suggests a strong decrease in employment, with PSP associated with staff reductions of 24 percent. And there is some evidence of an increase in investment per worker, although this is not confirmed by the matching procedure because of lack of data.

Connections and Output per Connection

The full panel estimation shows that PSP leads to an increase in both the number of residential electricity connections and the volume of electricity sold per connection. But the difference-in-differences estimation with matching, which pairs utilities chosen for PSP with the most comparable SOEs, confirms only an increase in connections for partial divestitures.

The results of the panel regression on the full sample show that in the post-PSP period the average number of connections for privately managed utilities increases by 2 percent over and above the change for publicly managed ones. The biggest increase, 21 percent, occurs for utilities granted as concessions. This result is intuitive: concession contracts often include explicit connection targets, and this type of PSP would be expected to lead to larger increases in connections. By contrast, the lack of increase in connections for full divestitures might be linked to the fact that network expansion is risky in developing countries and, depending on the tariff regime, not necessarily profitable.

Results for the full sample also show that the volume of electricity sold per connection increases by 3 percent for all PSP cases and by 16 percent for full divestitures, over and above the change for utilities without PSP.

The corrected results from the difference-in-differences estimation with matching, however, show no significant difference in the change in number of residential connections between utilities with PSP and those without, except for partial divestitures. For electricity sold per connection the positive effect of PSP does not hold, even for full divestitures.

[2] The reported result refers to partial divestitures, for which the most robust statistics exist.

Employment

Confirming a key finding of previous privatization research, the study finds strong evidence that employment decreases substantially as a result of PSP. This is shown by results throughout the range of model specifications, although results corrected by the matching procedure confirm this finding only for utilities that have been fully divested.

Some of the decrease in employment takes place in the transition period, implying that some restructuring is carried out to meet the expectations of investors. Still, for the aggregate sample, employment decreases by a mere 5 percent on average in the transition period, while it decreases by 24 percent in the post-PSP period. The disaggregated regressions suggest that the employment effect varies across types of PSP contracts: while employment decreases by 27 percent for full divestitures and 25 percent for partial ones, the results show no difference between utilities under concession or lease and management contracts and state-owned peers.

Private incentives in divestitures are most aligned with those under pure privatization, so this result is consistent with the privatization theory. Under the other types of contracts, it can be argued, private operators have less control over labor decisions, while employees have greater job protection.

Labor Productivity

For electricity utilities that were divested (fully or partially), there is strong evidence that PSP is associated with a significant increase in employment-driven labor productivity. In the full sample both the number of residential connections per worker and the volume of electricity sold per worker increase substantially more in the post-PSP period for utilities with PSP than for state-owned peers. Neither variable shows any significant change as a result of PSP during the transition period. This comes as no surprise because both variables are partially employment driven and most of the decrease in employment due to PSP occurs during the post-PSP period (see the previous section).

The labor productivity effect is not only highly significant at the 1 percent level, but also large: a 29 percent increase in residential connections per worker and a 32 percent increase in electricity sold per worker. But both effects hold only for divestitures: the number of connections per worker increases by 30 percent for full divestitures and by 32 percent for partial ones, while the volume of electricity sold per worker increases by 38 percent for full divestitures and by 33 percent for partial ones. For concessions and lease and management contracts both variables show either a decrease or no change, regardless of the econometric specification used. The corrected results with nearest-neighbor matching confirm the strong labor productivity effect, although the results hold firm throughout all specifications only for full divestitures.

Again the results are intuitive and aligned with the employment result: it is in divestitures that the analysis finds the largest reduction in staff numbers, and so labor productivity would be expected to increase. Because PSP has a weak effect or none at all on electricity sold per connection and on the number of residential connections, we can be reasonably certain that the labor productivity results are strongly employment driven. Moreover, it is in divestitures that the private operator has the most control over staffing decisions.

Collection Rate, Service Quality, and Distribution Losses

Conclusive results for the electricity sector show that PSP is associated with an increase in bill-collection rates and, for partial divestitures, improvements in electricity distribution losses.

Results for the full sample show that the collection rate increases substantially in the transition and post-PSP periods as a result of PSP. Moreover, it is not just divestiture (full or partial) that creates effective incentives to improve bill collection. There is evidence that concessions also do so (perhaps through contractual obligations to meet connection targets), confirming case-specific evidence. While the collection rate increases by an impressive 68 percent for partial divestitures and by 43 percent for full ones, over and above the change for equivalent SOEs, it increases by only a little less (40 percent) for concessions. The strong positive effect of PSP in general on the bill-collection rate is confirmed by the matching procedure.

The full panel estimation suggests that PSP has an adverse effect on service quality, showing an increase in annual supply interruptions for the transition period and for concessions. But these results are not confirmed by the matching procedure. Indeed, the corrected estimation with nearest-neighbor matching suggests that supply interruptions decrease for partial divestitures.

The full panel results show convincingly that PSP leads to a reduction in distribution losses, though only in divestitures (full and partial). The reduction is significant, however: 17 percent for full divestitures and 11 percent for partial ones. The improvement is confirmed in the matching procedure only for partial divestitures.

Finally, the full panel estimation suggests that PSP leads to a decrease in residential coverage, expressed as the percentage of households with connections, for both full divestitures and concessions and for the transition as well as the post-PSP period. This result cannot be confirmed by the matching procedure because too few data points are available. Still, the result merits further examination because of its implications for the assessment of PSP. Many experts have questioned the quality of data for this variable and the authors abstain from further interpretation due to concerns about the reliability of the data.

Investment and Price

The analysis finds some evidence for the electricity sector that divestitures result in greater increases in investment per worker and that concessions result in greater increases in consumer prices than observed in state-owned peers. But these results cannot be confirmed by the matching procedure because of insufficient data: disaggregation by type of contract leaves too few utilities with data for both the pre-PSP and the post-PSP period.

The specifications applied to the full sample indicate that PSP leads to an increase in investment per worker, as hoped by proponents of private involvement. Disaggregating by type of PSP shows that partial divestitures (in which investment per worker increases by 89 percent over and above the change for state-owned utilities) are largely responsible for this result. Because partial divestitures also experience a strong decrease in employment, it is impossible to say whether this result is driven by investment, employment, or some combination of the two. But given the strong employment effect reported, the result is likely to be driven at least in part by employment. This suggests a lack of investment for maintenance and expansion, which makes long-term improvement in service delivery less likely even if private sector involvement leads to operational improvements.

The panel regression on the full sample finds no overall effect of PSP on average residential tariffs (calculated as revenue divided by the volume of electricity sold for the residential sector), and disaggregation by type of PSP suggests that in the post-PSP period only concessions see greater increases than state-owned utilities, though by a considerable 35 percent. In addition, during the transition period there is a 6 percent increase in residential tariffs. But the nearest-neighbor matching procedure does not confirm these results; that is, the results do not survive the exclusion of utilities for which the study lacks at least one pre- and one post-PSP observation along with the exclusion of unsuitable comparators.

Water

For water services, striking results from the full panel estimation, confirmed by robust results in the difference-in-differences estimations, again show that PSP is associated with gains in performance and labor productivity. PSP leads to an estimated increase in residential connections of 12 percent, an increase in connections per worker of 54 percent, and an increase in water sold per worker of 18 percent (for concessions), over and above the change for SOEs. As in the electricity sector, employment decreases more strongly under private management, by 22 percent. And there is no evidence of an increase in investment or in retail tariffs following PSP.

Connections and Output per Connection

The analysis finds evidence that PSP leads to an expansion of water utilities' customer base, measured by the total number of residential connections. In the full panel estimation water utilities with PSP show an increase in the average number of connections beyond that for state-owned peers during both the transition period (8 percent) and the post-PSP period (12 percent). Disaggregating by type of contract suggests that these results can be attributed to all types except partial divestitures. The matching procedure suggests that concessions are the main driver of the results, confirming a significantly larger increase in the number of connections for concessions than for state-owned utilities.

In the full panel estimation water sold per connection also increases more for concessions (31 percent) than for state-owned utilities, but this result is not supported by the difference-in-differences estimation with matching.

Employment (Water and Sanitation)

In the water and sanitation sector, just as in the electricity sector, utilities with PSP exhibit the employment attrition effect predicted by the privatization literature, and the effect is strongest for full and partial divestitures.

The regression on the full sample yields results that are strikingly uniform across contract types: all (including concessions and lease and management contracts) show a decrease in employment in the post-PSP period beyond that for state-owned utilities, ranging from 20 percent for concessions to 34 percent for partial divestitures. Moreover, employment also decreases during the transition period, by 12 percent.

The difference-in-differences estimation with matching confirms that full and partial divestitures show a significantly larger decrease in employment than state-owned utilities, although it does not confirm the results for the aggregate or for concession and lease and management contracts. As noted, in the water sample the utilities with PSP are underrepresented compared with SOEs, so a matching procedure can yield greatly diverging results if the PSP and SOE groups in the full sample have very different characteristics. Nevertheless, the result from the matching procedure aligns with theory and mirrors the results in the electricity sector: PSP confers the incentive and the power to change employment numbers, particularly in divestitures.

Labor Productivity

PSP is associated with an increase in residential water connections per worker for partial divestitures, and the effect is likely to be driven largely by the drop in employment. Water sold per worker increases significantly for concessions.

In the full panel estimation all specifications suggest that residential connections per worker increase significantly for all types of PSP in both the transition and the post-PSP period. The increase in the post-PSP period ranges from 47 percent for concessions to 78 percent for partial divestitures. The difference-in-differences estimation with matching confirms that connections per worker increase for utilities with PSP and that the increase is driven mostly by partial divestitures (insufficient data hamper the confirmation of results for other types of contracts).

Results for the full sample show that water sold per worker increases only during the post-PSP period, not the transition period, rising by 18 percent for concessions, 40 percent for lease and management contracts, and 62 percent for partial divestitures. There are not enough observations to measure the effect for full divestitures. The difference-in-differences estimation can confirm the result only for concessions because there are too few observations to perform propensity score matching for other types of contracts, particularly divestitures.

Collection Rate, Service Quality, and Distribution Losses

The study finds no evidence for the water sector that PSP leads to an improvement in the bill-collection rate over and above that for state-owned counterparts and finds inconclusive evidence on its impact on residential coverage. And while it finds evidence that PSP leads to a significant decrease in water distribution losses and a significant improvement in service quality (measured by hours with water daily) for concessions and lease and management contracts, these results cannot be confirmed in the matching procedure because disaggregation leaves insufficient data.

Estimation results for the full panel show no impact of PSP on the collection rate. The matching procedure suggests no significant improvement beyond that for state-owned utilities, although yet again there is not enough information to answer the question for different types of PSP.

In the estimation for the full sample, residential coverage either decreases significantly or shows no significant change across all types of PSP, regardless of the level of private incentive implied. This result is somewhat surprising, and the fact that the results from the matching procedure either run in the opposite direction or are insignificant suggests that the data quality for this variable may be too poor for a conclusive result, mirroring the concerns in the electricity sector.

Results for operational performance and service quality, measured by water distribution losses and daily water service, are similarly inconclusive and hampered by the lack of data in the matching procedure. The panel regressions on the full sample suggest that PSP is associated with a significant reduction in distribution losses, an average of 23 percent for all types of PSP. Disaggregation by type shows that the decrease is significant only for concessions (24 percent) and lease and management contracts (20 percent). As noted, these results are not confirmed by the difference-in-differences specification with matching.

The panel regressions on the full sample show that daily water service increases by 41 percent on average in the post-PSP period for all types of PSP (38 percent for concessions and 49 percent for lease and management contracts) and by 15 percent in the transition period. But the difference-in-differences estimation with matching shows no significantly larger increase for utilities with PSP than for state-owned utilities in the post-PSP period, and the lack of sufficient data becomes obvious when the results are disaggregated by type of contract.

Investment and Price

The study finds no evidence for the water sector that the incentives from any form of private participation result in an increase in investment per worker. Nor does it find any evidence that PSP or any type of PSP leads to a larger increase in consumer prices than for state-owned utilities.

The results of the panel regression on the full sample suggest that investment per worker increases no more for water utilities with PSP than for state-owned utilities during the post-PSP period, despite the employment attrition documented. Nor is there any increase during the transition period. The difference-in-differences estimation with matching similarly shows no significant difference in investment per worker, though in this case because of lack of data.

Results for the full panel show no change in the average residential tariff (calculated as revenue divided by the volume of water sold for the residential sector) during either the transition or the post-PSP period, for any type of PSP contract. Results from the difference-in-differences estimation with matching, whether aggregated or disaggregated, show no significantly larger increase for utilities with PSP than for state-owned ones, although in most specifications there are not enough observations to evaluate this effect.

Sanitation

In the water and sanitation sample 75 percent of the 977 utilities provide both water distribution and sanitation services, while 1 percent operate only in the sanitation sector. Sanitation services provided by both mixed and pure sanitation companies are analyzed in the sanitation sample. The most striking effects of PSP from the full panel estimation are the estimated 37 percent increase in connections per worker and the 19 percent increase in residential coverage. There is also evidence of an increase in wastewater treated per worker following PSP. However, no panel result is confirmed in the matching procedure because of an overwhelming lack of data once the different restrictions of this approach are imposed.

Connections and Output per Connection

The study finds no significant effect of PSP on connections and output in the sanitation sector. In the full panel specification neither PSP in general, nor any type of PSP in particular, seems to have an effect on the number of sewerage connections or on output (wastewater treated) per connection. In the difference-in-differences estimation with matching, the number of usable utilities with any type of PSP is substantially smaller in the sanitation sample than in the electricity and water samples, leading to an inconclusive final assessment.

Labor Productivity

In the panel estimation for the full sample the number of residential sewerage connections per worker increases during both the transition and the post-PSP period, and in the post-PSP period it does so for all four types of contracts, with the size of the effect ranging from 27 percent for concessions to 59 percent for partial divestitures. But none of the effects can be confirmed in the matching procedure because of insufficient data.

Similarly, results for the full sample show that wastewater treated per worker increases by 33 percent on average in the post-PSP period for utilities with PSP, with partial divestitures driving this effect. Again because of insufficient data, however, the results cannot be confirmed in the matching procedure.

Coverage and Service Quality

The study finds a strong association of PSP with an increase in residential sewerage coverage, but no evidence that any type of PSP leads to an increase in the quality of sanitation services, measured by sewerage blockages per connection.

The finding that coverage increases as a result of PSP is among the strongest pieces of evidence from the analysis of the sanitation sample. Results for the full sample suggest that PSP leads to an increase in coverage of 18 percent during the transition period and to an increase for all types of PSP except partial divestitures in the post-PSP period, with the effect ranging from 20 percent for lease and management contracts to 40 percent for full divestitures.

No conclusive result is found for service quality as measured by sewerage blockages. When utilities are matched in the difference-in-differences procedure, the inadequacy of the data again precludes any conclusion.

6.

CONCLUSION

The results of the study corroborate earlier findings about the impact of introducing the private sector in formerly state-managed companies. Moreover, they provide a statistical robustness missing from research based on case studies and small samples. They also confirm the premise that private incentives lead to cost savings and efficiency improvements.

The results suggest two conclusions. First, both private sector participation (PSP) and the type of PSP matter, with greater degrees of private participation associated with stronger gains in productivity and service quality. Second, some previous studies may have overstated or understated the true impact of PSP as a result of the nonrandom selection of utilities for PSP and ex-ante differences between utilities with PSP and state-owned enterprise (SOE) comparators. The two methodological improvements in this study—disaggregation by type of contract and nearest-neighbor matching of utilities based on propensity score—correct for this bias.

The study finds robust evidence in the global sample that PSP has a strong positive effect on several measures of performance: the average number of residential water connections increases by 12 percent, electricity sold per worker by 32 percent, residential coverage in sanitation services by 19 percent, and the bill-collection rate in the electricity sector by 45 percent. In addition, distribution losses in electricity decrease by 11 percent, and hours of daily water service increase by 41 percent. These effects—differences in averages between the pre-PSP and the post-PSP period—occur over five years or more and are over and above the change for similar SOEs. No aspect of service examined deteriorates under PSP, although the evidence of an improvement in service does not withstand all tests either: no statistically significant change occurs in annual interruptions in power supply or in sewerage blockages per connection.

While most of the positive effects are observed during the post-PSP period, some efficiency gains are realized during the transition period, probably as governments try to make utilities more attractive to investors or as a result of managerial anticipation. In most cases the impact during the transition period is weaker than that observed in the post-PSP period. But in a few cases the transition effect is both substantial and comparable to that in the post-PSP period: in the electricity sample the collection rate increases by about 20 percent during the transition period, compared with 45 percent during the post-PSP period. And in some cases the transition effect runs in the opposite direction: for example, electricity distribution losses increase during the transition period (by about 11 percent) before dropping in the post-PSP years. Some of these unexpected effects may be due to corrections in the base data for the utility, which often occur in preparation for the entry of a private operator.

While the analysis suggests that PSP across the board is associated with a robust positive effect on some measures of performance, disaggregation reveals differences across types of PSP. In the electricity sector, utilities that underwent full or partial divestiture show the biggest gains (except in the bill-collection rate, which also increases significantly for concessions); in water and sanitation services, utilities under concessions and lease or management contracts realize the biggest gains. The differences between the sectors in results by type of contract may reflect the fact that in the water sector divestitures are few and almost always partial, with the state retaining control over the assets. The results also suggest that contractual obligations traditionally associated with concessions, leases, and management contracts, such as improving service quality and expanding coverage, may indeed be producing measurable results.

An important finding is the strong labor effect of PSP: average employment decreases by 24 percent in the electricity sector and by 22 percent in the water sector over and above the change for state-owned peers. The observed staff reductions improve utilities' productivity; the study finds evidence of an employment-driven increase in labor productivity in all sectors. Moreover, the staff reductions are small relative to the national labor force; only in a few exceptional cases do the reductions in a utility represent more than 2 percent of national unemployment.[1] But that does not take away from the

[1] For a detailed discussion of the relative size of staff reductions, see also McKenzie and Mookherjee (2003).

seriousness with which governments need to address the employment question. Mitigating measures need to be put into place early on. The question for policy makers is one of trading off the social costs of reform against the social costs of inaction.

The study finds no robust evidence that private control of management changes either investment or the average residential tariff. Because the efficiency gains from PSP would translate into lower costs for the operator, why is there no sign of the lower costs translating into greater investment or lower prices? Keeping in mind that investment and tariff data are notoriously difficult to compare and analyze, several interpretations can be considered.

First, services may initially be so underpriced that even significant efficiency gains do not produce a financial equilibrium or justify price reductions, at least in the residential sector. The global evidence of underpricing of utility services in developing countries, particularly water services, makes this a plausible explanation (Foster and Yepes 2006). In this scenario an absence of PSP would have led to even larger losses for the utility and thus even larger outlays by the government.

Second, the private operator may reap all the gains through profits, passing on none of the cost savings to consumers. Given the young regulatory environments in developing countries, which often lack sufficient capacity for supervising public-private contracts, this possibility needs to be considered. Detailed profit data and more in-depth research are needed to confirm or invalidate this argument.

Third, it could be argued that no increase in investment by the private operator would be expected where the operator has responsibility only for operations and not for assets, as in lease or management contracts. But where the assets remain under public ownership, the utility-specific data should show maintenance and capital outlays by the government as well as the private operator. The apparent lack of increase in either private or public investment is a concern. Indeed, for companies whose assets governments have chosen to keep in public hands, a shortfall in public investment raises doubts about the long-term sustainability of the operational improvements achieved under private management.

APPENDIX A

CORE INDICATORS

Data on both qualitative and quantitative indicators were collected for each utility in the sample. The qualitative set covers utility- and country-level characteristics. It contains information on the type of private sector participation (PSP) contract and the year of entry by the private sector. The qualitative indicators are used mostly to determine whether and for which period a utility can be considered a PSP case and as control variables for the type of utility and other differences among utilities.

The quantitative indicators include measures of outputs (for example, water and electricity sold), inputs (for example, number of workers), physical capital (approximated by, for example, the customer base), labor productivity (defined as output per worker), operational performance (for example, level of network losses or bill-collection rate), service quality (for example, daily water supply and average frequency of interruptions in electricity per year), and average prices (calculated as revenues divided by volume sold).

Table A.1 summarizes the indicators used. The utility-level indicators were collected on a yearly basis for 13 years, from 1992 to 2004, and, where available, for 2005. In a number of cases data earlier than 1992 were available and also were included in the panel. Table A.2 shows the observations of core indicators by year. As a result of problems in data collection and verification, there are many gaps in the data; nevertheless, the overall size and range of the sample permits robust statistical analysis. Tables A.3–A.5 give the summary statistics for the variables used in the analysis for the electricity, water, and sanitation sectors.

Table A.1 Description of Core Indicators

Indicator	Electricity distribution	Water distribution and sanitation services
Output	• Electricity sold to residential and nonresidential customers per connection (MWh)	• Water sold to residential and nonresidential customers per connection (cubic meters) • Wastewater treated per connection (cubic meters)
Labor	• Employees	• Employees, water and sanitation
Labor productivity	• Residential connections per worker • Electricity sold per worker (MWh)	• Residential connections per worker, water and sanitation • Water sold per worker (cubic meters) • Wastewater treated per worker (cubic meters)
Operational performance	• Electricity lost in distribution (% of electricity produced and purchased)	• Water lost in distribution (% of water produced)
Service quality	• Annual supply interruptions	• Hours with water daily • Sewerage blockages per sewerage connection
Investment	• Total annual investment (CAPEX) per worker (US$)	• Total annual investment (CAPEX) per worker (US$)
Capital, capacity	• Residential and nonresidential connections	• Residential and nonresidential connections, water and sanitation
Coverage	• Potential residential customers covered (% of households)	• Potential residential customers covered (% of population)
Collection rate	• Outstanding bills collected (%)	• Outstanding bills collected (%)
Price	• Average residential tariff (US$) calculated as revenue divided by volume sold	• Average residential tariff (US$) calculated as revenue divided by volume sold

Source: Authors' compilation.
Note: MWh = megawatt-hours. CAPEX = capital expenditures.

Table A.2 Utility-Year Observations, by Sector

Year	Electricity	Water and sanitation	Both sectors
1973	1	0	1
1974	1	0	1
1975	1	0	1
1976	1	0	1
1977	1	0	1
1978	1	0	1
1979	1	0	1
1980	1	2	3
1981	1	2	3
1982	1	2	3
1983	1	2	3
1984	1	2	3
1985	2	2	4
1986	4	2	6
1987	33	2	35
1988	37	2	39
1989	39	3	42
1990	60	18	78
1991	71	36	107
1992	133	36	169
1993	134	40	174
1994	141	57	198
1995	175	174	349
1996	203	230	433
1997	217	423	640
1998	224	538	762
1999	230	588	818
2000	238	755	993
2001	238	799	1,037
2002	233	758	991
2003	212	710	922
2004	124	581	705
2005	31	80	111
Total	2,791	5,844	8,635

Source: Authors' calculations.

Note: Utility-year observations are the number of utilities for which at least one of the core indicators (see tables A.3–A.5) was observed in a given year.

Table A.3 Summary Statistics for Electricity

Variable	Observations	Mean	Median	Standard deviation	Minimum	Maximum
Residential connections	2,024	472,795	250,296	573,491	9,700	3,130,902
Electricity sold per connection (MWh)	2,258	6	4	10	0.5	198
Employees	1,847	2,464	1,272	3,407	43	30,800
Electricity sold per worker (MWh)	1,816	1,787	1,303	1,637	50	16,743
Residential connections per worker	1,650	370	283	315	3	3,825
Residential coverage (% of households)[a]	414	84	99	25	5	100
Collection rate (%)[b]	431	78	85	25	20	104
Electricity lost in distribution (%)	2,030	17	15	9	1	91
Annual supply interruptions	742	382	20	1,707	3	18,331
Total annual investment (CAPEX) per worker (US$)	453	14,794	8,811	16,312	61	89,096
Average residential tariff per MWh (US$)	1,538	85	83	41	4	276

Source: Authors' calculations.
Note: Monetary amounts are in 2005 U.S. dollars. All values are annual. MWh = megawatt-hours; CAPEX = capital expenditures.
a. The quality of the coverage data for electricity was judged to be unreliable.
b. Collection rates may exceed 100 percent because of debts collected for previous years.

Table A.4 Summary Statistics for Water

Variable	Observations	Mean	Median	Standard deviation	Minimum	Maximum
Residential connections	2,477	128,496	30,651	251,925	752	1,575,457
Water sold per connection (cubic meters)	4,553	1,144	225	12,888	2	713,333
Employees	5,224	357	168	507	5	3,179
Water sold per worker (cubic meters)	4,743	46,020	30,649	176,749	208	11,400,000
Residential connections per worker	2,378	265	216	221	14	3,938
Residential coverage (% of population)	4,214	79	87	22	19	100
Collection rate (%)[a]	2,699	97	100	8	51	103
Water lost in distribution (%)	4,499	33	31	17	1	100
Hours with water daily	2,625	20	24	6	4	24
Total annual investment (CAPEX) per worker (US$)	1,762	7,631	2,678	16,660	0	323,698
Average residential tariff per cubic meter (US$)	1,916	1	0	1	0	7

Source: Authors' calculations.
Note: Monetary amounts are in 2005 U.S. dollars. All values are annual. CAPEX = capital expenditures.
a. Collection rates may exceed 100 percent because of debts collected for previous years.

Table A.5 Summary Statistics for Sanitation

Variable	Observations	Mean	Median	Standard deviation	Minimum	Maximum
Residential connections	1,827	133,556	31,307	402,344	10	5,663,544
Wastewater treated per connection (cubic meters)	1,514	511	199	1,022	0	13,839
Wastewater treated per worker (cubic meters)	676	101,011	68,029	112,611	273	925,208
Residential connections per worker	1,717	180	145	173	0	3,063
Residential coverage (% of population)	2,786	63	70	31	0	100
Sewerage blockages per connection	1,709	0	0	2	0	54

Source: Authors' calculations.
Note: All values are annual.

Figures A.1–A.3 plot the main indicators underlying the study, allowing readers to visualize the difference between the PSP and SOE samples over time. The figures show the mean and median values to give an impression of the importance of extreme values in the data series. The threshold (time = 0) is defined as the year when the private contract became operational for firms with PSP. For firms without PSP it is defined as the average year PSP was introduced in the country or region.

Figure A.1 Time Trends of Core Indicators for Electricity

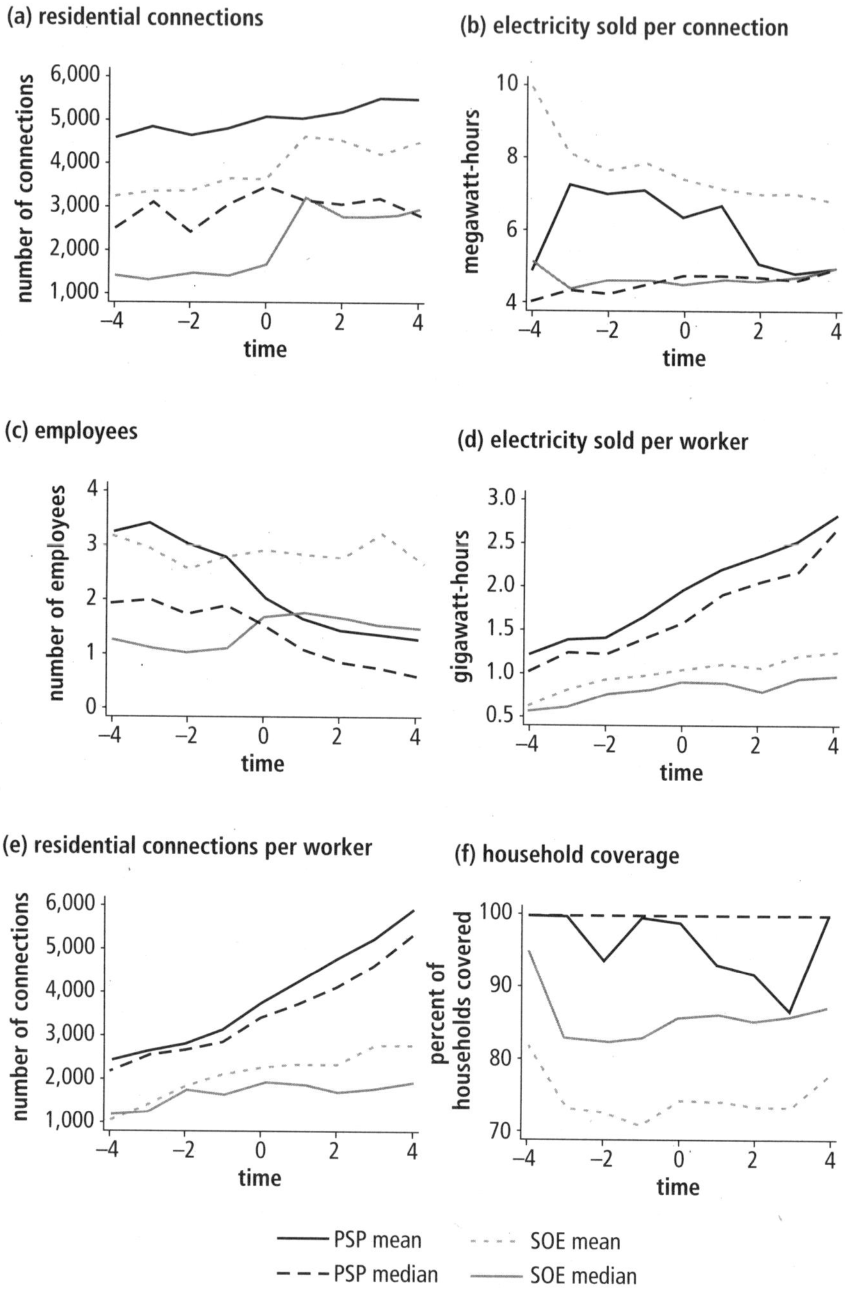

Figure A.1 Time Trends of Core Indicators for Electricity *(Continued)*

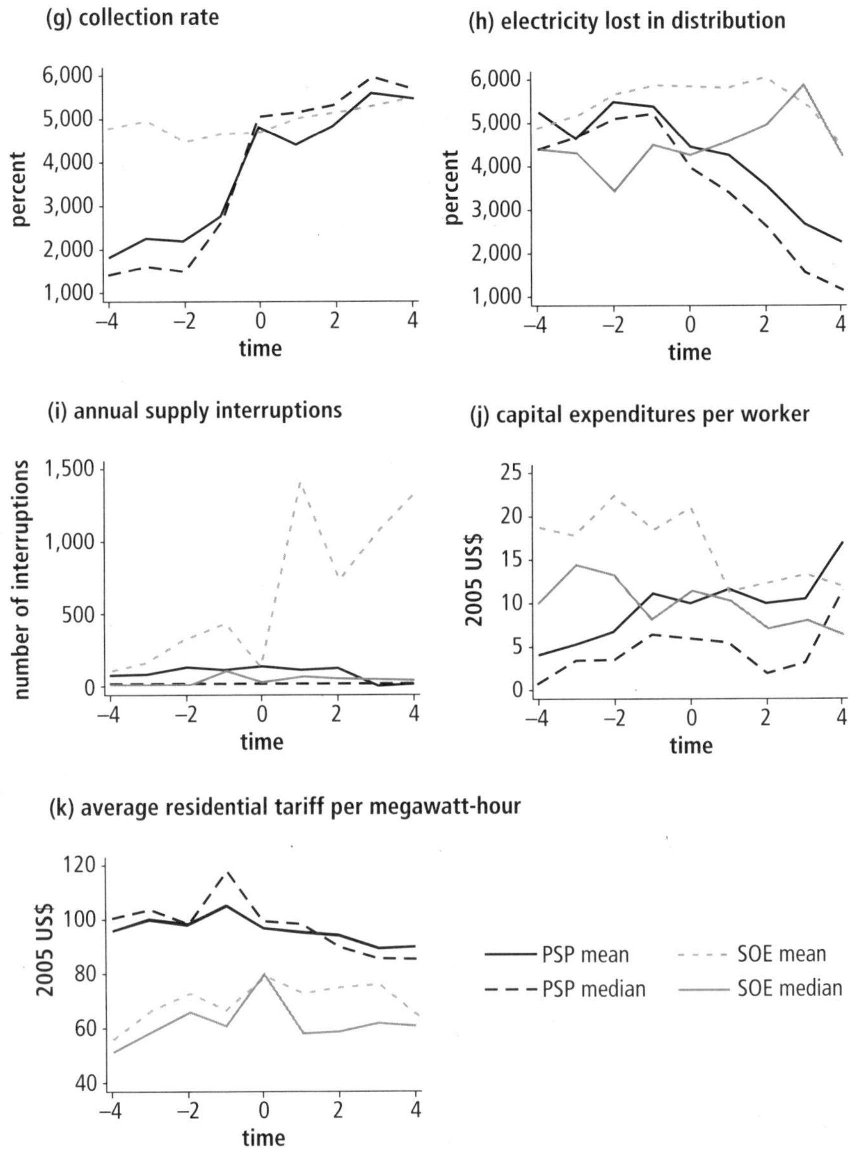

Source: Authors' calculations.
Note: The quality of the coverage data for electricity was judged to be too unreliable to be used in the analysis.

Figure A.2 Time Trends of Core Indicators for Water

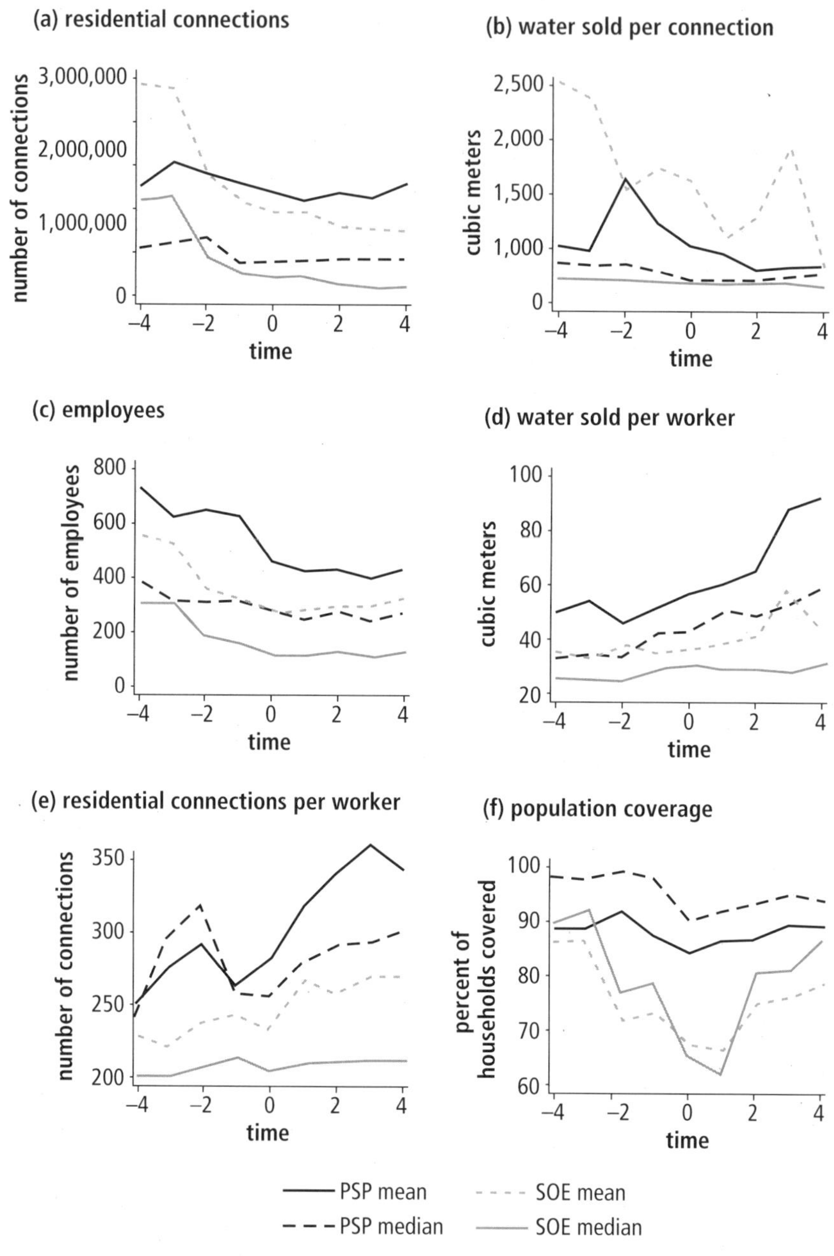

Figure A.2 Time Trends of Core Indicators for Water *(Continued)*

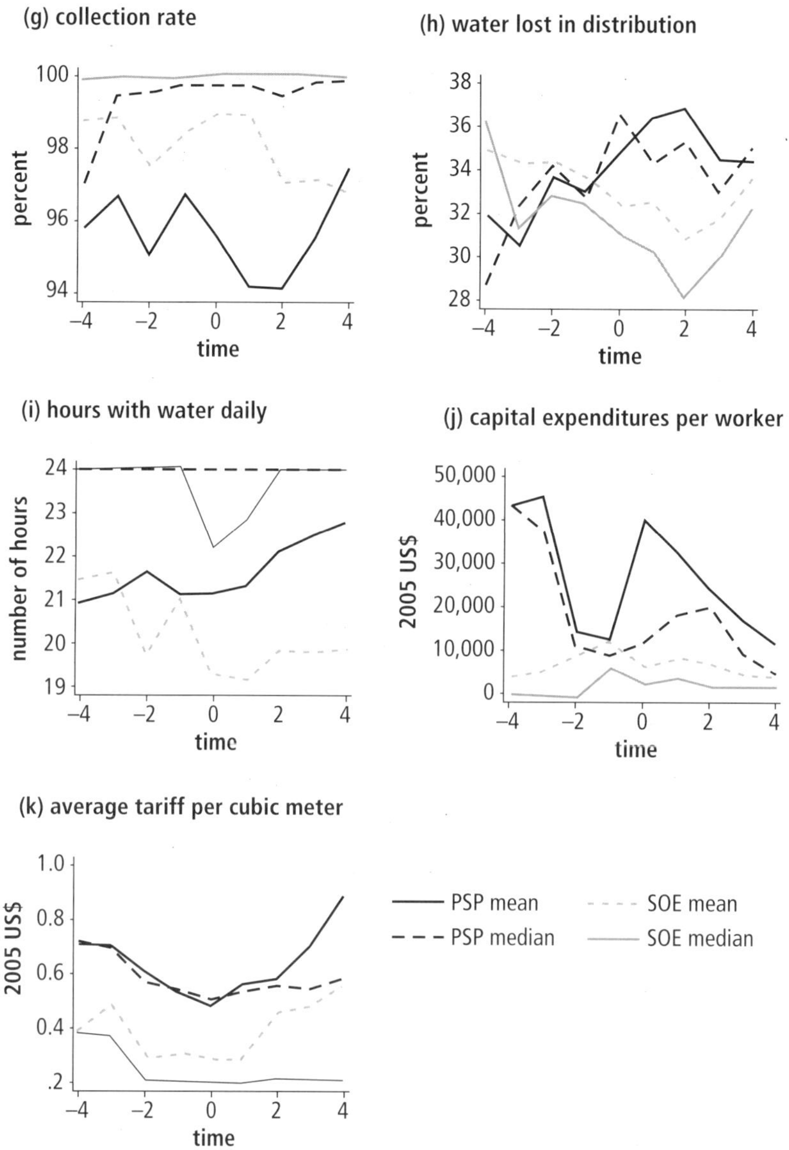

Source: Authors' calculations.

Figure A.3 Time Trends of Core Indicators for Sanitation

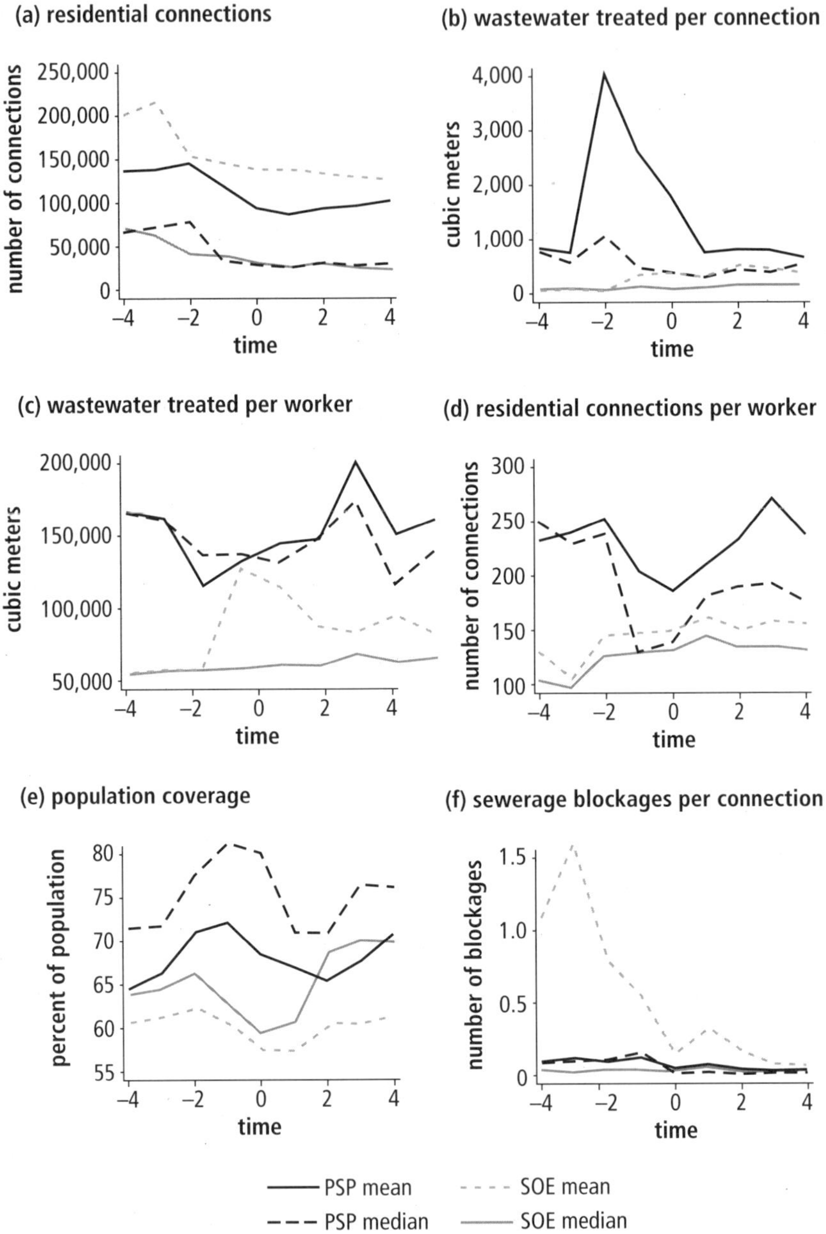

Source: Authors' calculations.

APPENDIX B

VARIABLE SOURCES, CONSTRUCTION, AND ESTIMATIONS

All estimations are based on the software package Stata 9.2.

Dollar-denominated monetary variables (CAPEX and average tariffs) are calculated as follows:

$$X_t^{REAL} = \frac{X_t^{NOMINAL}}{FXrate \times \text{CPI}}, \tag{B.1}$$

where *FXrate* is the exchange rate between the local currency and the U.S. dollar on December 31 and CPI is the U.S. consumer price index with the base year 2005.

The non-firm-level variables are from the World Bank Development Data Platform.

The exchange rate and consumer price index are International Monetary Fund estimates taken from the World Bank Development Data Platform.

APPENDIX C

COX PROPORTIONATE HAZARD ESTIMATES

The estimation of the Cox proportionate hazard model justifies the use of propensity score matching because it demonstrates that there is indeed a lack of randomness in the choice of private sector participation (PSP); in other words, governments do not choose utilities for PSP randomly. The results, reported in tables C.1 and C.2, show the Cox proportionate hazard estimation of the probability of a utility ending up with any form of PSP (column 1) and the probability of a utility being selected for different types of contracts (columns 2–4 and 2–5, respectively).[1]

The results for the electricity sector show that the probability of a utility being selected for PSP is not independent of a change in gross domestic product (GDP) per capita (an increase in GDP per capita makes it more likely that the utility will be chosen for PSP) and a change in unemployment (an increase in unemployment makes it less likely). When the contract types are disaggregated, the results show that utilities with a larger customer base are more likely to be chosen for PSP and that electricity lost in distribution plays an additional role in the type of PSP selected.[2] In addition, GDP per capita, inflation, and changes in inflation play a role in the choice of full divestiture. The assumption of a random selection of utilities for PSP is therefore rejected.

The estimation results for the water sector are somewhat less straightforward because fewer data are available for disaggregation by type of contract,

[1] There is not enough information to perform the analysis for lease and management contracts in the electricity sector.

[2] This procedure and the result are comparable to those of Brown, Earle, and Telegdy (2006), who find that privatization is correlated with firm-specific output and productivity before privatization, although the sign varies by country.

Table C.1 Cox Proportionate Hazard Estimates of Being Subjected to Various Types of PSP in Electricity

Variable	(1) PSP	(2) DF	(3) DP	(4) Conc
Residential connections	—	0.426	0.047	−0.02
		(0.300)	(0.024)**	(0.112)
Employees	−0.052	—	—	—
	(0.050)			
Electricity lost in distribution	−0.023	−0.146	−0.012	−0.059
	(0.016)	(0.076)*	(0.019)	(0.053)
GDP per capita	−0.024	−23.561	−0.081	−1.071
	(0.087)	(8.340)***	(0.092)	(0.482)**
Δ GDP per capita	1	85.814	1.464	0.002
	(0.467)**	(30.798)***	(0.770)*	(1.818)
Unemployment	−0.054	0.969	0.04	—
	(0.041)	(0.369)***	(0.045)	
Δ Unemployment	−0.194	3.49	−0.018	—
	(0.106)*	(1.627)**	(0.126)	
Inflation	−0.003	−0.817	−0.003	−0.192
	(0.003)	(0.324)**	(0.008)	(0.132)
Δ Inflation	0.003	−0.024	0.004	−0.009
	(0.003)	(0.012)**	(0.007)	(0.120)
Observations	692	907	901	1,326

Source: Authors' calculations.

Note: Standard errors are in parentheses. PSP is a dummy variable equal to 1 if the utility was subjected to PSP, in and after the PSP year, and equal to 0 otherwise. DF is a dummy variable equal to 1 if the utility was subjected to full divestiture, in and after the PSP year, and equal to 0 otherwise. DP is a dummy variable equal to 1 if the utility was subjected to partial divestiture, in and after the PSP year, and equal to 0 otherwise. Conc is a dummy variable equal to 1 if the utility was subjected to concession, in and after the PSP year, and equal to 0 otherwise. — = insufficient data are available.

* Significant at 10 percent level.

** Significant at 5 percent level.

*** Significant at 1 percent level.

Table C.2 Cox Proportionate Hazard Estimates of Being Subjected to Various Types of PSP in Water and Sanitation

Variable	(1) PSP	(2) DF	(3) DP	(4) Conc	(5) LMC
Residential connections	—	—	0.168 (0.094)*	—	—
Employees	—	−18.192 (10.860)*	—	—	—
Water sold	0.009 (0.002)***	—	—	0.007 (0.003)**	0.015 (0.005)***
GDP per capita	0.193 (0.084)**	1.237 (0.477)***	0.484 (0.374)	0.284 (0.064)***	−0.301 (0.386)
Δ GDP per capita	0.154 (0.38)	−0.514 (3.752)	−0.09 (1.511)	−0.133 (0.279)	1.193 (1.912)
Unemployment	0.004 (0.036)	−0.54 (0.281)*	−0.276 (0.236)	0.029 (0.024)	0.1 (0.131)
Δ Unemployment	0.04 −0.116	—	—	−0.006 −0.062	−0.079 −0.329
Inflation	−0.068 (0.029)**	−0.338 (0.369)	−0.211 (0.164)	−0.048 (0.018)***	0.005 (0.066)
Δ Inflation	0.043 (0.026)*	—	—	−0.001 −0.001	−0.001 −0.059
Observations	4,000	4,814	2,359	10,446	4,318

Source: Authors' calculations.

Note: Standard errors are in parentheses. PSP is a dummy variable equal to 1 if the utility was subjected to PSP, in and after the PSP year, and equal to 0 otherwise. DF is a dummy variable equal to 1 if the utility was subjected to full divestiture, in and after the PSP year, and equal to 0 otherwise. DP is a dummy variable equal to 1 if the utility was subjected to partial divestiture, in and after the PSP year, and equal to 0 otherwise. Conc is a dummy variable equal to 1 if the utility was subjected to concession, in and after the PSP year, and equal to 0 otherwise. LMC is a dummy variable equal to 1 if the utility was subjected to a lease or management contract, in and after the PSP year, and equal to 0 otherwise. — = insufficient data are available.

* Significant at 10 percent level.

** Significant at 5 percent level.

*** Significant at 1 percent level.

particularly for divestitures. But the assumption of random selection for PSP can be rejected for this sector as well. Utilities that sell more water are more likely to be chosen for PSP, and this is confirmed for concessions and lease and management contracts. As in the electricity sector, utilities with more residential connections are more likely to be chosen for PSP; those with fewer employees also are more likely to be chosen. And full divestitures and concessions are more likely to occur when GDP per capita is higher than the sample average.

Overall, customer base, employment size, inflation, unemployment, and GDP per capita in the pre-PSP period seem with fair certainty to influence the probability of PSP in both the water and the electricity sector. For the purposes of the study, however, it is irrelevant whether utilities with larger size, higher labor productivity, or some other characteristic are more likely to be offered for PSP. What matters is that utilities with certain characteristics influencing their performance have a larger equilibrium probability of being selected for PSP: the endogeneity concern is very real. In addition, the results suggest that pre-PSP characteristics may determine the kind of PSP contract chosen for a utility, conditional on being selected for PSP in the first place.

Consequently, matching the utilities with PSP in a nearest-neighbor matching procedure to state-owned utilities that are similar across the range of utility-level characteristics defined by the estimation of the Cox proportionate hazard model is a valid empirical exercise. Adopting this way of proceeding will correct the PSP impact results for bias caused by pre-PSP characteristics.

APPENDIX D

REGRESSION RESULTS

Table D.1 Effect of PSP on Performance in Electricity

Model	(1) Residential connections	(2) Electricity sold per connection	(3) Employees	(4) Electricity sold per worker	(5) Residential connections per worker	(6) Residential coverage	(7) Collection rate	(8) Electricity lost in distribution	(9) Annual supply interruptions	(10) CAPEX per worker	(11) Average residential tariff
Model A: Log levels with a random effect for utility (full sample)											
PSP	0.025	0.032	−0.278	0.287	0.262	−0.093	0.287	−0.158	−0.023	0.356	0.035
	(0.014)*	(0.016)*	(0.028)***	(0.029)***	(0.028)***	(0.029)***	(0.060)***	(0.027)***	(0.075)	(0.191)*	(0.020)*
TD	0.010	−0.021	−0.048	0.020	0.044	−0.081	0.119	0.085	0.248	0.275	0.055
	(0.011)	(0.014)	(0.023)**	(0.024)	(0.024)*	(0.020)***	(0.052)**	(0.022)***	(0.060)***	(0.154)*	(0.020)***
Observations	2,109	2,258	1,924	1,816	1,650	431	448	2,030	773	434	1,477
R^2	0.32	0.64	0.58	0.62	0.71	0.90	0.74	0.40	0.69	0.73	0.79
Model B: Log levels with a fixed effect for utility and a firm-specific time trend (full sample)											
PSP	0.024	0.028	−0.274	0.274	0.252	−0.093	0.374	−0.135	0.092	0.429	0.012
	(0.013)*	(0.017)*	(0.027)***	(0.029)***	(0.029)***	(0.030)***	(0.074)***	(0.028)***	(0.074)	(0.234)*	(0.033)
TD	0.009	−0.023	−0.047	0.009	0.037	−0.08´	0.178	0.101	0.326	0.294	0.055
	(0.011)	(0.014)*	(0.022)**	(0.024)	(0.024)	(0.020)***	(0.060)***	(0.023)***	(0.059)***	(0.180)	(0.029)*
Observations	2,109	2,258	1,924	1,816	1,650	431	448	2,030	773	434	1,477
R^2	0.7	0.06	0.49	0.74	0.76	0.19	0.37	0.12	0.3	0.05	0.32
Model C: Difference-in-differences (utilities with at least one pre- and one post-PSP observation)											
PSP	0.029	0.102	−0.387	0.488	0.319	−0.174	0.525	−0.215	−0.251	0.873	−0.246
	(0.045)	(0.054)*	(0.095)***	(0.123)***	(0.118)***	(0.102)*	(0.136)***	(0.070)***	(0.199)	(0.591)	(0.113)**
Observations	109	113	86	83	73	27	20	115	29	12	58
R^2	0.00	0.03	0.16	0.16	0.09	0.11	0.45	0.08	0.06	0.18	0.08

Model D: Difference-in-differences with matching (utilities with at least one pre- and one post-PSP observation)											
PSP	0.025	−0.015	−0.332	0.407	0.347	—	0.490	−0.093	−0.105	—	−0.113
	(0.073)	(0.083)	(0.127)***	(0.164)***	(0.134)***		(0.227)**	(0.136)	(0.228)		(0.154)
Observations	102	94	68	66	64		10	88	28		49

Source: Authors' calculations.

Note: Standard errors are in parentheses. All regressions in models A and B include fixed effects for country and year (unreported). Model D uses pre-PSP, utility-specific values for connections and employment to calculate the propensity score. TD = transition dummy variable; — = insufficient data are available.

* Significant at 10 percent level.

** Significant at 5 percent level.

*** Significant at 1 percent level.

Table D.2 Effect of PSP on Performance in Electricity, by Type of PSP Contract

Model	(1) Residential connections	(2) Electricity sold per connection	(3) Employees	(4) Electricity sold per worker	(5) Residential connections per worker	(6) Residential coverage	(7) Collection rate	(8) Electricity lost in distribution	(9) Annual supply interruptions	(10) CAPEX per worker	(11) Average residential tariff
Model A: Log levels with a random effect for utility (full sample)											
Full divestiture	−0.027	0.148	−0.337	0.333	0.275	−0.1	0.272	−0.226	−0.221	0.372	0.041
	(0.019)	(0.022)***	(0.040)***	(0.042)***	(0.041)***	(0.034)***	(0.078)***	(0.038)***	(0.124)*	(0.257)	(0.027)
Partial divestiture	0.028	−0.015	−0.288	0.291	0.289	0.417	0.303	−0.134	−0.06	0.461	0.021
	(0.015)*	(0.018)	(0.030)***	(0.031)***	(0.030)***	(0.334)	(0.085)***	(0.030)***	(0.078)	(0.254)*	(0.022)
Concession	0.195	0.01	0.118	−0.026	−0.234	−0.08	0.306	−0.122	0.554	0.488	0.292
	(0.038)***	(0.043)	(0.096)	(0.100)	(0.103)**	(0.044)*	(0.107)***	(0.079)	(0.181)***	(0.335)	(0.080)***
Lease or management contract	0.104	−0.024	0.017	−1.477	−1.228	—	0.174	0.289	5.495	−2.111	0.554
	(0.125)	(0.092)	(0.252)	(0.547)***	(0.474)***		(0.216)	(0.254)	(1.222)***	(0.838)**	(0.231)**
TD	0.001	−0.007	−0.057	0.026	0.053	−0.081	0.113	0.085	0.222	0.286	0.059
	(0.011)	(0.014)	(0.023)**	(0.024)	(0.024)**	(0.020)***	(0.053)**	(0.022)***	(0.060)***	(0.152)*	(0.020)***
Observations	2,109	2,258	1,924	1,816	1,650	431	448	2,030	773	434	1,477
R^2	0.33	0.64	0.58	0.62	0.72	0.90	0.74	0.41	0.70	0.74	0.79
Model B: Log levels with a fixed effect for utility and a firm-specific time trend (full sample)											
Full divestiture	−0.028	0.145	−0.317	0.319	0.26	−0.1	0.356	−0.189	−0.068	0.271	0.008
	(0.018)	(0.022)***	(0.039)***	(0.043)***	(0.043)***	(0.035)***	(0.091)***	(0.040)***	(0.126)	(0.317)	(0.043)
Partial divestiture	0.027	−0.018	−0.289	0.282	0.281	—	0.516	−0.117	0.048	0.634	−0.01
	(0.014)*	(0.018)	(0.029)***	(0.031)***	(0.030)***		(0.126)***	(0.031)***	(0.077)	(0.314)**	(0.035)
Concession	0.193	0.012	0.114	−0.036	−0.246	−0.08	0.336	−0.11	0.615	0.512	0.3
	(0.037)***	(0.043)	(0.092)	(0.099)	(0.102)**	(0.045)*	(0.109)***	(0.080)	(0.175)***	(0.339)	(0.082)***

Lease or management contract	0.103	−0.024	0.023	—	—	—	0.216	0.312	—	−1.24	—
	(0.121)	(0.091)	(0.245)				(0.221)	(0.254)		(0.923)	
TD	0.001	−0.008	−0.055	0.016	0.046	−0.081	0.182	0.102	0.298	0.285	0.054
	(0.011)	(0.014)	(0.022)**	(0.024)	(0.024)*	(0.020)***	(0.062)***	(0.023)***	(0.059)***	(0.182)	(0.028)*
Observations	2,109	2,258	1,924	1,816	1,650	431	448	2,030	773	434	1,477
R^2	0.71	0.09	0.5	0.74	0.77	0.19	0.37	0.12	0.31	0.06	0.33
Model C: Difference-in-differences (utilities with at least one pre- and one post-PSP observation)											
Full divestiture	−0.027	0.259	−0.557	0.585	0.611	−0.168	1.177	−0.127	0.049	—	−0.063
	(0.075)	(0.094)***	(0.141)***	(0.212)***	(0.153)***	(0.156)	(0.111)***	(0.104)	(0.351)		(0.177)
Observations	55	62	46	43	33	23	14	73	8		29
R^2	0.00	0.11	0.26	0.16	0.34	0.05	0.90	0.02	0.0		0.0
Partial divestiture	0.048	0.055	−0.435	0.566	0.383	—	0.1	−0.232	−0.368	1.674	−0.315
	(0.047)	(0.060)	(0.091)***	(0.105)***	(0.105)***		(0.111)	(0.078)***	(0.202)*	(0.961)	(0.115)***
Observations	87	89	70	67	60		14	87	23	8	50
R^2	0.01	0.01	0.25	0.31	0.19		0.06	0.09	0.14	0.34	0.13
Concession	0.026	0.079	0.324	−0.267	−0.594	−0.179	0.48	−0.366	0.093	0.473	0.137
	(0.112)	(0.119)	(0.163)*	(0.205)	(0.154)***	(0.135)	(0.125)***	(0.130)***	(0.200)	(0.661)	(0.304)
Observations	47	55	40	37	30	24	18	61	10	10	25
R^2	0.00	0.01	0.09	0.05	0.35	0.07	0.48	0.12	0.03	0.06	0.01
Lease or management contract	—	−0.129	—	—	—	—	—	—	—	—	—
		(0.328)									
Observations		48									
R^2		0.00									

(continued)

Table D.2 Effect of PSP on Performance in Electricity, by Type of PSP Contract *(Continued)*

Model	(1) Residential connections	(2) Electricity sold per connection	(3) Employees	(4) Electricity sold per worker	(5) Residential connections per worker	(6) Residential coverage	(7) Collection rate	(8) Electricity lost in distribution	(9) Annual supply interruptions	(10) CAPEX per worker	(11) Average residential tariff
Model D: Difference-in-differences with matching (utilities with at least one pre- and one post-PSP observation)											
Full divestiture	−0.039	0.156	−0.637	0.851	0.679	—	—	−0.065	—	—	0.148
	(0.085)	(0.137)	(0.201)***	(0.382)**	(0.258)***			(0.178)			(0.109)
Observations	29	29	21	20	15			32			11
Partial divestiture	0.117	0.003	−0.157	0.207	0.185	—	—	−0.155	−0.332	—	−0.075
	(0.054)**	(0.083)	(0.197)	(0.135)*	(0.170)			(0.111)*	(0.186)**		(0.190)
Observations	68	64	48	47	47			48	16		30
Concession	0.121	−0.238	0.023	−0.494	−0.101	—	—	−0.134	—	—	—
	(0.168)	(0.183)	(0.070)	(0.153)***	(0.188)			(0.241)			
Observations	18	20	8	8	8			17			
Lease or management contract	—	—	—	—	—	—	—	—	—	—	—
Observations											

Source: Authors' calculations.

Note: Standard errors are in parentheses. All regressions in models A and B include fixed effects for country and year as well as a transition dummy variable (unreported). Model D uses pre-PSP values for the relevant variables for each type of contract to calculate the propensity score (see table A.3). TD = transition dummy variable; — = insufficient data are available.

* Significant at 10 percent level.

** Significant at 5 percent level.

*** Significant at 1 percent level.

Table D.3 Effect of PSP on Performance in Water

Model	(1) Residential connections	(2) Electricity sold per connection	(3) Employees	(4) Electricity sold per worker	(5) Residential connections per worker	(6) Residential coverage	(7) Collection rate	(8) Electricity lost in distribution	(9) Annual supply interruptions	(10) CAPEX per worker	(11) Average residential tariff
Model A: Log levels with a random effect for utility (full sample)											
PSP	0.123	0.184	−0.231	0.275	0.38	−0.053	0.002	−0.127	0.291	0.654	0.079
	(0.023)***	(0.070)***	(0.028)***	(0.064)***	(0.043)***	(0.022)**	(0.019)	(0.059)**	(0.049)***	(0.233)***	(0.044)*
TD	0.079	0.057	−0.117	0.077	0.208	−0.065	−0.017	0.018	0.103	0.362	0.084
	(0.020)***	(0.069)	(0.025)***	(0.064)	(0.039)***	(0.020)***	(0.019)	(0.057)	(0.042)**	(0.272)	(0.040)**
Observations	2,580	4,553	5,441	4,743	2,378	4,389	2,812	4,499	2,734	1,691	1,839
R^2	0.10	0.32	0.18	0.54	0.16	0.37	0.43	0.12	0.34	0.40	0.76
Model B: Log levels with a fixed effect for utility and a firm-specific time trend (full sample)											
PSP	0.117	0.205	−0.25	0.239	0.43	−0.065	0.032	−0.26	0.341	0.665	0.001
	(0.021)***	(0.085)**	(0.028)***	(0.085)***	(0.049)***	(0.025)***	(0.025)	(0.079)***	(0.054)***	(0.486)	(0.052)
TD	0.075	0.078	−0.131	0.056	0.249	−0.073	0.009	−0.085	0.138	0.293	0.037
	(0.019)***	(0.080)	(0.024)***	(0.079)	(0.044)***	(0.021)***	(0.025)	(0.070)	(0.046)***	(0.474)	(0.045)
Observations	2,580	4,553	5,441	4,743	2,378	4,389	2,812	4,499	2,734	1,691	1,839
R^2	0.49	0.09	0.09	0.03	0.29	0.07	0.01	0.02	0.05	0.21	0.33
Model C: Difference-in-differences (utilities with at least one pre- and one post-PSP observation)											
PSP	0.223	0.01	−0.332	0.017	0.504	0.038	0.023	−0.137	0.274	0.654	0.276
	(0.052)***	(0.089)	(0.078)***	(0.160)	(0.088)***	(0.081)	(0.024)	(0.129)	(0.187)	(1.262)	(0.216)
Observations	86	71	124	78	82	42	66	89	18	8	29
R^2	0.18	0.00	0.13	0.00	0.29	0.01	0.01	0.01	0.12	0.04	0.06

(continued)

Table D.3 Effect of PSP on Performance in Water (Continued)

Model	(1) Residential connections	(2) Electricity sold per connection	(3) Employees	(4) Electricity sold per worker	(5) Residential connections per worker	(6) Residential coverage	(7) Collection rate	(8) Electricity lost in distribution	(9) Annual supply interruptions	(10) CAPEX per worker	(11) Average residential tariff
Model D: Difference-in-differences with matching (utilities with at least one pre- and one post-PSP observation)											
PSP	0.324	0.154	0.020	0.182	0.921	−0.083	0.037	−0.085	0.110	—	−0.023
	(0.192)*	(0.186)	(0.242)	(0.328)	(0.298)***	(0.307)	(0.026)	(0.191)	(0.110)		(0.655)
Observations	6	16	22	18	6	7	6	20	9		11

Source: Authors' calculations.
Note: Standard errors are in parentheses. All regressions in models A and B include fixed effects for country and year (unreported). Model D uses pre-PSP, utility-specific values for connections and water sold to calculate the propensity score. TD = transition dummy variable; — = insufficient data are available.
* Significant at 10 percent level.
** Significant at 5 percent level.
*** Significant at 1 percent level.

Table D.4 Effect of PSP on Performance in Water, by Type of PSP Contract

Model	(1) Residential connections	(2) Electricity sold per connection	(3) Employees	(4) Electricity sold per worker	(5) Residential connections per worker	(6) Residential coverage	(7) Collection rate	(8) Electricity lost in distribution	(9) Annual supply interruptions	(10) CAPEX per worker	(11) Average residential tariff
Model A: Log levels with a random effect for utility (full sample)											
Full divestiture	0.162	1.356	−0.251	1.183	0.378	−0.145	—	−0.507	0.13	—	−0.015
	(0.049)***	(0.500)***	(0.077)***	(0.400)***	(0.100)***	(0.049)***		(0.344)	(0.251)		(0.120)
Partial divestiture	0	−0.179	−0.396	0.559	0.551	−0.126	−0.014	−0.131	0.148	1.114	0.035
	(0.039)	(0.246)	(0.058)***	(0.231)**	(0.076)***	(0.046)***	(0.070)	(0.236)	(0.146)	(0.722)	(0.079)
Concession	0.145	0.223	−0.201	0.229	0.348	−0.011	0.008	−0.137	0.273	0.604	0.066
	(0.026)***	(0.076)***	(0.032)***	(0.072)***	(0.048)***	(0.025)	(0.019)	(0.066)**	(0.055)***	(0.245)**	(0.053)
Lease or management contract	0.179	0.118	−0.224	0.322	0.337	−0.105	−0.021	−0.093	0.355	0.756	0.173
	(0.038)***	(0.108)	(0.043)***	(0.091)***	(0.068)***	(0.036)***	(0.027)	(0.089)	(0.065)***	(0.535)	(0.069)**
TD	0.092	0.073	−0.111	0.07	0.201	−0.06	−0.018	0.015	0.105	0.355	0.09
	(0.020)***	(0.069)	(0.025)***	(0.064)	(0.039)***	(0.020)***	(0.019)	(0.057)	(0.043)**	(0.273)	(0.040)**
Observations	2,580	4,553	5,441	4,743	2,378	4,389	2,812	4,499	2,734	1,691	1,839
R^2	0.10	0.32	0.18	0.54	0.16	0.37	0.43	0.12	0.34	0.40	0.76
Model B: Log levels with a fixed effect for utility and a firm-specific time trend (full sample)											
Full divestiture	0.16	—	−0.241	—	0.431	−0.155	—	—	—	—	−0.023
	(0.046)***		(0.075)***		(0.106)***	(0.051)***					(0.132)
Partial divestiture	−0.006	−0.271	−0.415	0.484	0.574	−0.133	0.011	−0.326	0.177	1.04	−0.001
	(0.036)	(0.278)	(0.057)***	(0.278)*	(0.078)***	(0.047)***	(0.072)	(0.314)	(0.174)	(0.751)	(0.080)
Concession	0.137	0.268	−0.223	0.169	0.385	−0.022	0.035	−0.278	0.324	0.467	−0.027
	(0.024)***	(0.091)***	(0.031)***	(0.092)*	(0.055)***	(0.027)	(0.026)	(0.087)***	(0.061)***	(0.532)	(0.062)

(continued)

Table D.4 Effect of PSP on Performance in Water, by Type of PSP Contract (Continued)

Model	(1) Residential connections	(2) Electricity sold per connection	(3) Employees	(4) Electricity sold per worker	(5) Residential connections per worker	(6) Residential coverage	(7) Collection rate	(8) Electricity lost in distribution	(9) Annual supply interruptions	(10) CAPEX per worker	(11) Average residential tariff
Lease or management contract	0.177 (0.036)***	0.133 (0.126)	−0.241 (0.042)***	0.337 (0.111)***	0.413 (0.078)***	−0.118 (0.039)***	0.013 (0.035)	−0.218 (0.108)**	0.396 (0.068)***	1.45 (0.963)	0.099 (0.083)
TD	0.087 (0.019)***	0.106 (0.081)	−0.125 (0.024)***	0.039 (0.080)	0.236 (0.044)***	−0.067 (0.021)***	0.007 (0.025)	−0.089 (0.071)	0.141 (0.046)***	0.213 (0.496)	0.044 (0.046)
Observations	2,580	4,553	5,441	4,743	2,378	4,389	2,812	4,499	2,734	1,691	1,839
R^2	0.49	0.09	0.09	0.03	0.29	0.07	0.01	0.02	0.05	0.21	0.33
Model C: Difference-in-differences (utilities with at least one pre- and one post-PSP observation)											
Full divestiture	0.372 (0.127)***	—	−0.189 (0.210)	—	0.459 (0.191)**	−0.059 (0.049)	—	—	—	—	−0.099 (0.483)
Observations	66		90		66	15					13
R^2	0.12		0.01		0.08	0.10					0.00
Partial divestiture	0.069 (0.089)	−0.786 (0.232)***	−0.374 (0.166)**	0.288 (0.461)	0.452 (0.151)***	−0.004 (0.041)	—	—	—	0.27 (1.810)	0.431 (0.350)
Observations	69	61	92	69	68	16				7	16
R^2	0.01	0.16	0.05	0.01	0.12	0.00				0.00	0.10
Concession	0.276 (0.073)***	0.169 (0.097)*	−0.405 (0.095)***	0.153 (0.195)	0.53 (0.124)***	0.119 (0.038)***	0.023 (0.024)	−0.331 (0.153)**	0.418 (0.281)	1.038 (1.810)	0.322 (0.294)
Observations	73	67	110	74	72	3[illegible]	66	85	12	7	19
R^2	0.17	0.04	0.14	0.01	0.21	0.25	0.01	0.05	0.18	0.06	0.07

Lease or management contract	0.208 (0.110)*	−0.097 (0.141)	−0.084 (0.152)	−0.345 (0.279)	0.586 (0.236)**	−0.233 (0.191)	—	0.203 (0.197)	0.214 (0.079)**	—	0.056 (0.848)
Observations	67	63	93	71	65	16		82	13		11
R^2	0.05	0.01	0.00	0.02	0.09	0.10		0.01	0.40		0.00
Model D: Difference-in-differences with matching (utilities with at least one pre- and one post-PSP observation)											
Full divestiture	—	—	−0.439 (0.076)***	—	—	—	—	—	—	—	—
Observations			5								
Partial divestiture	0.340 (0.511)	—	−0.589 (0.178)***	—	0.615 (0.207)***	−0.049 (0.037)	—	—	—	—	—
Observations	8		7		7	6					
Concession	0.365 (0.218)*	−0.042 (0.194)	0.083 (0.198)	0.932 (0.300)***	0.403 (0.401)	0.269 (0.101)**	0.037 (0.026)	−0.451 (0.366)	—	—	0.042 (0.566)
Observations	6	9	14	12	6	5	6	13			10
Lease or management contract	—	0.096 (0.287)	−0.001 (0.245)	0.258 (0.782)	—	−0.778 (0.616)	—	0.327 (0.278)	0.183 (0.183)	—	—
Observations		5	8	6		4		8	6		

Source: Authors' calculations.

Note: Standard errors are in parentheses. All regressions in models A and B include fixed effects for country and year and a transition dummy variable (unreported). Model D uses pre-PSP values for the relevant variables for each type of contract to calculate the propensity score (see table A.4). TD = transition dummy variable; — = insufficient data are available.

* Significant at 10 percent level.

** Significant at 5 percent level.

*** Significant at 1 percent level.

Table D.5 Effect of PSP on Performance in Sanitation

Model	(1) Residential connections	(2) Wastewater treated per connection	(3) Wastewater treated per worker	(4) Residential connections per worker	(5) Residential coverage	(6) Sewerage blockages per connection
Model A: Log levels with a random effect for utility (full sample)						
PSP	0.009	−0.066	0.275	0.258	0.16	0.288
	(0.060)	(0.173)	(0.109)**	(0.073)***	(0.035)***	(0.361)
TD	0.039	−0.048	−0.001	0.126	0.150	−0.269
	(0.052)	(0.170)	(0.099)	(0.066)*	(0.030)***	(0.351)
Observations	1,827	1,514	676	1,717	2,786	1,497
R^2	0.05	0.49	0.62	0.17	0.26	0.24
Model B: Log levels with a fixed effect for utility and a firm-specific time trend (full sample)						
PSP	0.008	−0.24	0.284	0.313	0.177	0.552
	(0.058)	(0.236)	(0.117)**	(0.079)***	(0.037)***	(0.587)
TD	0.042	−0.214	0.004	0.175	0.163	−0.114
	(0.050)	(0.223)	(0.105)	(0.071)**	(0.031)***	(0.512)
Observations	1,827	1,514	676	1,717	2,786	1,497
R^2	0.29	0.01	0.16	0.28	0.09	0.01

Model C: Difference-in-differences (utilities with at least one pre- and one post-PSP observation)						
PSP	0.077	−0.678	1.607	0.411	0.223	—
	(0.130)	(0.619)	(0.291)	(0.153)***	(0.145)	
Observations	71	39	3	69	29	
R^2	0.01	0.03	0.97	0.10	0.08	
Model D: Difference-in-differences with matching (utilities with at least one pre- and one post-PSP observation)						
PSP	—	—	—	—	0.044	—
					(0.109)	
Observations					7	

Source: Authors' calculations.
Note: Standard errors are in parentheses. All regressions in models A and B include fixed effects for country and year (not reported). Model D uses pre-PSP, utility-specific values for connections and water sold to calculate the propensity score. TD = transition dummy variable; — = insufficient data are available.
* Significant at 10 percent level.
** Significant at 5 percent level.
*** Significant at 1 percent level.

Table D.6 Effect of PSP on Performance in Sanitation, by Type of PSP Contract

Model	(1) Residential connections	(2) Wastewater treated per connection	(3) Wastewater treated per worker	(4) Residential connections per worker	(5) Residential coverage	(6) Sewerage blockages per connection
Model A: Log levels with a random effect for utility (full sample)						
Full divestiture	0.038	—	—	0.241	0.307	−0.857
	(0.116)			(0.146)*	(0.078)***	(1.238)
Partial divestiture	0.021	−0.164	0.742	0.434	0.071	1.017
	(0.091)	(0.479)	(0.171)***	(0.115)***	(0.055)	(1.221)
Concession	−0.016	−0.034	0.121	0.192	0.177	0.413
	(0.069)	(0.177)	(0.118)	(0.084)**	(0.039)***	(0.388)
Lease or management contract	0.056	−0.389	0.147	0.267	0.161	−0.065
	(0.101)	(0.457)	(0.725)	(0.115)**	(0.055)***	(0.556)
TD	0.033	−0.034	−0.096	0.111	0.16	−0.299
	(0.053)	(0.172)	(0.102)	(0.067)*	(0.030)***	(0.353)
Observations	1,827	1,514	676	1,717	2,786	1,497
R^2	0.05	0.49	0.62	0.17	0.26	0.24

Model B: Log levels with a fixed effect for utility and a firm-specific time trend (full sample)						
Full divestiture	0.052	—	—	0.285	0.334	—
	(0.110)			(0.149)*	(0.079)***	
Partial divestiture	0.011	−0.317	0.734	0.463	0.081	—
	(0.086)	(0.500)	(0.173)***	(0.116)***	(0.056)	
Concession	−0.021	−0.196	0.104	0.239	0.198	0.871
	(0.066)	(0.245)	(0.127)	(0.090)***	(0.041)***	(0.656)
Lease or management contract	0.074	−0.521	—	0.351	0.181	0.204
	(0.098)	(0.495)		(0.124)***	(0.056)***	(0.668)
TD	0.036	−0.188	−0.111	0.156	0.175	−0.042
	(0.051)	(0.227)	(0.109)	(0.071)**	(0.031)***	(0.516)
Observations	1,827	1,514	676	1,717	2,786	1,497
R^2	0.29	0.01	0.18	0.28	0.09	0.01
Model C: Difference-in-differences (utilities with at least one pre- and one post-PSP observation)						
Full divestiture	0.143	—	—	0.289	0.42	—
	(0.296)			(0.328)	(0.154)**	
Observations	58			58	9	
R^2	0.00			0.01	0.51	

(continued)

Table D.6 Effect of PSP on Performance in Sanitation, by Type of PSP Contract *(Continued)*

Model	(1) Residential connections	(2) Wastewater treated per connection	(3) Wastewater treated per worker	(4) Residential connections per worker	(5) Residential coverage	(6) Sewerage blockages per connection
Partial divestiture	0.166	—	1.607	0.41	0.135	—
	(0.230)		(0.291)	(0.284)	(0.054)**	
Observations	60		3	59	12	
R^2	0.01		0.97	0.04	0.39	
Concession	−0.022	−0.402	—	0.482	0.28	—
	(0.210)	(0.874)		(0.254)*	(0.191)	
Observations	61	38		60	18	
R^2	0.00	0.01		0.06	0.12	
Lease or management contract	0.049	−0.954	—	0.422	0.077	—
	(0.363)	(0.874)		(0.402)	(0.078)	
Observations	57	38		57	11	
R^2	0.00	0.03		0.02	0.10	

Model D: Difference-in-differences with matching (utilities with at least one pre- and one post-PSP observation)						
Full divestiture	—	—	—	—	—	—
Observations						
Partial divestiture	−0.437	—	—	—	—	—
	(0.943)					
Observations	7					
Concession	—	—	—	—	0.175	—
	(0.134)					
Observations					4	
Lease or management contract	—	—	—	—	−0.113	—
					(0.094)	
Observations					4	

Source: Authors' calculations.

Note: Standard errors are in parentheses. All regressions in models A and B include fixed effects for country and year and a transition dummy variable (not reported). Model D uses pre-PSP values for the relevant variables for each type of contract to calculate the propensity score (see table A.5). TD = transition dummy variable; — = insufficient data are available.

* Significant at 10 percent level.

** Significant at 5 percent level.

*** Significant at 1 percent level.

BIBLIOGRAPHY

Abdala, Manuel, and Pablo Spiller. 1999. *Instituciones, contratos, y regulación en Argentina.* Buenos Aires: Grupo Editorial (for Fundación Gobierno y Sociedad).

Aghion, Philippe, Olivier Blanchard, and Robin Burgess. 1994. "The Behavior of State Firms in Eastern Europe, Pre-Privatization." *European Economic Review* 38 (June): 1327–49.

Andres, Luis. 2004. "The Impact of Privatization on Firms in the Infrastructure Sector in Latin American Countries." PhD dissertation, University of Chicago.

Andres, Luis, Vivien Foster, and José Luis Guasch. 2006. "The Impact of Privatization on the Performance of the Infrastructure Sector: The Case of Electricity Distribution in Latin American Countries." Policy Research Working Paper 3936. World Bank, Washington, DC.

Andres, Luis, Vivien Foster, José Luis Guasch, and T. Haven. Forthcoming. *The Impact of Private Sector Participation in Infrastructure: Lights and Shadows.* Latin American Development Forum Series. Washington, DC: World Bank.

Auriol, Emmanuelle, and Pierre Picard. 2006. *Infrastructure and Public Utilities Privatization in Developing Countries.* CEPR Discussion Paper 6018. London: Centre for Economic Policy Research.

Berg, Sanford, Chen Lin, and Valeriy Tsaplin. 2005. "Regulation of State-Owned and Privatized Utilities: Ukraine Electricity Distribution Company Performance." *Journal of Regulatory Economics* 28 (3): 259–87.

Berg, Sanford, and William T. Muhairwe. 2006. "Healing an Organization: High Performance Lessons from Africa." Draft. Public Utility Research Center, University of Florida, Gainesville.

Bortolotti, Bernardo, Juliet D'Souza, Marcella Fantini, and William L. Megginson. 2001. "Sources of Performance Improvements in Privatized Firms: A Clinical Study of the Global Telecommunications Industry." Department of Finance Working

Paper. University of Oklahoma, Norman; FEEM Working Paper 26. Fondazione Eni Enrico Mattei, Milan.

Boubakri, Narjess, and Jean-Claude Cosset. 1998. "The Financial and Operating Performance of Newly Privatized Firms: Evidence from Developing Countries." *Journal of Finance* 53 (3): 1081–110.

Boycko, Maxim, Andrei Shleifer, and Robert Vishny. 1993. "Privatizing Russia." Brookings *Papers on Economic Activity* 2: 139–92.

Bradburn, Ralph. 1992. "Privatization of Natural Monopoly Public Enterprises: The Regulation Issues." Country Economics Department Paper 864. World Bank, Washington, DC.

Briceño-Garmendia, Cecilia. 2004. "Empirical Literature on Private Participation in Infrastructure: An Annotated Survey and Its Profile." Infrastructure Advisory Services, World Bank, Washington, DC.

Brown, J. David, and John Earle. 1999. "Privatization and Restructuring in Russia: New Evidence from Panel Data on Industrial Enterprises." Paper presented at the Stockholm Institute of Transition Economics and East European Economies (SITE), Russian-European Centre for Economic Policy (RECEP) conference, Stockholm. December.

Brown, J. David, John Earle, and Almos Telegdy. 2006. "The Productivity Effects of Privatization: Longitudinal Estimates from Hungary, Romania, Russia, and Ukraine." *Journal of Political Economy* 114 (1): 61–99.

Card, David, and Alan Krueger. 1993. "Minimum Wages and Employment: A Case Study of the Fast-Food Industry in New Jersey and Pennsylvania." NBER Working Paper 4509. National Bureau of Economic Research, Cambridge, MA.

Chisari, Omar, Antonio Estache, and Carlos Romero. 1999. "Winners and Losers from Utility Privatization in Argentina: Lessons from a General Equilibrium Model." *World Bank Economic Review* 13 (2): 357–78.

Clarke, George, Claude Ménard, and Ana Maria Zuluaga. 2000. "The Welfare Effects of Private Sector Participation in Guinea's Urban Water Supply." Policy Research Working Paper 2361. World Bank, Washington, DC.

Delmon, Jeffrey. 2006. *Approaches to Private Participation in Water Services: A Toolkit.* Washington, DC: World Bank.

Dewenter, Kathryn, and Paul Malatesta. 1997. "Public Offerings of State-Owned and Privately Owned Enterprises: An International Comparison." *Journal of Finance* 52 (4): 1659–79.

———. 2001. "State-Owned and Privately Owned Firms: An Empirical Analysis of Profitability, Leverage, and Labor Intensity." *American Economic Review* 91 (1): 320–34.

Earle, John, and Saul Estrin. 1997. *After Voucher Privatization: The Structure of Corporate Ownership in Russian Manufacturing Industry.* CEPR Discussion Paper 1736. London: Centre for Economic Policy Research.

Ehrlich, Isaac, Georges Gallais-Hamonno, Zhiqiang Liu, and Randall Lutter. 1994. "Productivity Growth and Firm Ownership: An Analytical and Empirical Investigation." *Journal of Political Economy* 102 (5): 1006–38.

Estache, Antonio, Andres Gomez-Lobo, and Danny Leipziger. 2001. "Utilities Privatization and the Poor: Lessons and Evidence from Latin America." *World Development* 29 (July): 1179–98.

Estache, Antonio, and Martin Rossi. 2002. "How Different Is the Efficiency of State and Private Water Companies in Asia?" *World Bank Economic Review* 16 (1): 139–48.

Fink, Carsten, Aaditya Mattoo, and Randeep Rathindran. 2002. "An Assessment of Telecommunications Reform in Developing Countries." Policy Research Working Paper 2909. World Bank, Washington, DC.

Foster, Vivien, and Tito Yepes. 2006. "Is Cost Recovery a Feasible Objective for Water and Electricity? The Latin American Experience." Policy Research Working Paper 3943. World Bank, Washington, DC.

Frydman, Roman, Cheryl Grey, Marek Hessel, and Andrzej Rapaczynski. 1999. "When Does Privatization Work? The Impact of Private Ownership on Corporate Performance in the Transition Economies." *Quarterly Journal of Economics* 114 (4): 1153–91.

Galal, Ahmed, Leroy Jones, Pankaj Tandon, and Ingo Vogelsang. 1994. *Welfare Consequences of Selling State Enterprises.* Oxford: Oxford University Press.

Galiani, Sebastian, Paul Gertler, and Ernesto Schargrodsky. 2005. "Water for Life: The Impact of the Privatization of Water Services on Child Mortality." *Journal of Political Economy* 113 (1): 83–120.

Gasmi, Farid, Paul Noumba, and Laura Recuero Virto. 2006. "Political Accountability and Regulatory Performance in Infrastructure Industries: An Empirical Analysis." Policy Research Working Paper 4101. World Bank, Washington, DC.

Gassner, Katharina, Alexander Popov, and Nataliya Pushak. 2008. "An Empirical Assessment of Private Sector Participation in Electricity and Water Distribution in Developing and Transition Economies." PPIAF, Washington, DC. http://www.ppiaf.org/content/view/269/434/.

Griliches, Zvi, and Jerry A. Hausman. 1986. "Errors in Variables in Panel Data." *Journal of Econometrics* 31 (1): 93–118.

Groom, Eric, Jonathan Halpern, and David Ehrhardt. 2006. *Explanatory Notes on Key Topics in the Regulation of Water and Sanitation Services.* Water Supply and Sanitation Sector Board Discussion Paper 6. Washington, DC: World Bank.

Halvorsen, Robert, and Raymond Palmquist. 1980. "The Interpretation of Dummy Variables in Semilogarithmic Equations." *American Economic Review* 70 (3): 474–75.

Haskel, Jonathan, and Stefan Szymanksi. 1993. "Privatization, Liberalization, Wages, and Employment: Theory and Evidence for the UK." *Economica* 60 (238): 161–81.

Heckman, James, and V. Joseph Hotz. 1989. "Choosing among Alternative Nonexperimental Methods for Estimating the Impact of Social Programs: The Case of Manpower Training (in Applications and Case Studies)." *Journal of the American Statistical Association* 84 (408): 862–74.

Heckman, James, and Richard Robb. 1986. "Alternative Methods for Estimating the Impact of Interventions." In *Longitudinal Analysis of Labor Market Data,* ed. James Heckman and Burton Singer. Cambridge, U.K.: Cambridge University Press.

Heckman, James, Hidehiko Ichimura, and Petra Todd. 1998. "Matching as an Econometric Evaluation Estimator." *Review of Economic Studies* 65 (April): 261–94.

Hodge, Graeme. 1999. *Privatization: An International Performance Review.* Boulder, CO: Westview Press.

IEA (International Energy Agency). 2002. *World Energy Outlook: Energy and Poverty.* Paris: IEA. http://www.worldenergyoutlook.org/weo/pubs/weo2002/EnergyPoverty.pdf.

La Porta, Rafael, and Florencio López-de-Silanes. 1999. "The Benefits of Privatization: Evidence from Mexico." *Quarterly Journal of Economics* 114 (4): 1193–242.

Laurin, Claude, and Yves Bozec. 2001. "Privatization and Productivity Improvement: The Case of Canadian National." *Transportation Research Part E: Logistics and Transportation Review* 37 (5): 355–74.

Lipton, David, Jeffrey Sachs, and Lawrence Summers. 1990. "Privatization in Eastern Europe: The Case of Poland." *Brookings Papers on Economic Activity* 2: 293–341.

McKenzie, David, and Dilip Mookherjee. 2003. "The Distributive Impact of Privatization in Latin America: Evidence from Four Countries." *Economia* 3 (2): 161–233.

Megginson, William, Robert Nash, and Matthias van Randenborgh. 1994. "The Financial and Operating Performance of Newly Privatized Firms: An Empirical Analysis." *Journal of Finance* 49 (2): 403–52.

Megginson, William, and Jeffry Netter. 2001. "From State to Market: A Survey of Empirical Studies on Privatization." *Journal of Economic Literature* 39 (2): 321–89.

Nellis, John. 2003. "Privatization in Latin America." Working Paper 31. Center for Global Development, Washington, DC.

Newbery, David M., and Michael G. Pollitt. 1997. "The Restructuring and Privatisation of Britain's Cegb—Was It Worth It?" *Journal of Industrial Economics* 45 (3): 269–303.

Picot, Arnold, and Thomas Kaulman. 1989. "Comparative Performance of Government-Owned and Privately Owned Industrial Corporations: Empirical Results from Six Countries." *Journal of Institutional and Theoretical Economics* 145 (2): 298–316.

Primeaux, Walter J. Jr. 1986. *Direct Electric Utility Competition: The Natural Monopoly Myth.* New York: Praeger.

Ramamurti, Ravi. 1996. "The New Frontier of Privatization." In *Privatizing Monopolies: Lessons from the Telecommunications and Transport Sectors in Latin America,* ed. Ravi Ramamurti. Baltimore: Johns Hopkins University Press.

Ravallion, Martin. 2001. "The Mystery of the Vanishing Benefits: An Introduction to Impact Evaluation." *World Bank Economic Review* 15 (1): 115–40.

Roland, Gerard, and Khalid Sekkat. 2000. "Managerial Career Concerns, Privatization, and Restructuring in Transitional Economies." *European Economic Review* 44 (December): 1857–72.

Ros, Agustin. 1999. "Does Ownership or Competition Matter? The Effects of Telecommunications Reform on Network Expansion and Efficiency." *Journal of Regulatory Economics* 15 (1): 65–92.

Ros, Agustin, and Aniruddha Banerjee. 2000. "Telecommunications Privatization and Tariff Rebalancing: Evidence from Latin America." *Telecommunications Policy* 24 (3): 233–52.

Rosenbaum, Paul, and Donald Rubin. 1983. "The Central Role of the Propensity Score in Observational Studies for Causal Effects." *Biometrica* 70 (April): 41–55.

Shleifer, Andrei. 1998. "State versus Private Ownership." *Journal of Economic Perspectives* 12 (4): 133–50.

Vining, Aidan, and Anthony Boardman. 1992. "Ownership versus Competition: Efficiency in Public Enterprise." *Public Choice* 73 (2): 205–39.

Viscusi, W. Kip, John Vernon, and Joseph Harrington. 2000. *Economics of Regulation and Antitrust.* Cambridge, MA: MIT Press.

Wallsten, Scott. 2001. "An Econometric Analysis of Competition, Privatization, and Regulation in Telecommunications Markets in Africa and Latin America." *Journal of Industrial Economics* 49 (1): 1–19.

WHO (World Health Organization) and UNICEF (United Nations Children's Fund). 2004. *Meeting the MDG Drinking Water and Sanitation Target: A Mid-Term Assessment of Progress.* Geneva: WHO; New York: UNICEF.

INDEX

Figures, notes, and tables are indicated by *f*, *n*, and *t*, respectively.

D

E

Q

R

S

T

ECO-AUDIT

Environmental Benefits Statement

The World Bank is committed to preserving endangered forests and natural resources. The Office of the Publisher has chosen to print *Does Private Sector Participation Improve Performance in Water and Electricity?* on recycled paper with 30 percent postconsumer fiber in accordance with the recommended standards for paper usage set by the Green Press Initiative, a nonprofit program supporting publishers in using fiber that is not sourced from endangered forests. For more information, visit www.greenpressinitiative.org.

Saved:

- 10 trees
- 7 million British thermal units of total energy
- 860 pounds of net greenhouse gases
- 3,570 gallons of waste water
- 458 pounds of solid waste

green press INITIATIVE